What every primary school teacher should know about vocabulary

Jannie van Hees and Paul Nation

What every primary school teacher should know about vocabulary

Jannie van Hees and Paul Nation

NZCER PRESS

NZCER PRESS
New Zealand Council for Educational Research
PO Box 3237
Wellington
New Zealand

www.nzcer.org.nz

© Jannie van Hees and Paul Nation 2017

ISBN 978-1-947509-66-5

No part of the publication may be copied, stored or communicated in any form by any means (paper or digital), including recording or storing in an electronic retrieval system, without the written permission of the publisher.
Education institutions that hold a current licence with Copyright Licensing New Zealand may copy from this book in strict accordance with the terms of the CLNZ Licence.

A catalogue record for this book is available from the National Library of New Zealand

Designed by Smartwork Creative Ltd

Contents

Chapter 1 **Introduction**	1
Overview	1
The book in a nutshell	2
What should teachers do?	5
Chapter 2 **The nature of vocabulary**	7
Basic ideas	7
Vocabulary size and word frequency	8
Using word frequencies	9
Subject matter vocabulary	15
Further reading	17
Resources	17
Chapter 3 **Knowing vocabulary**	18
Knowing a word	18
Beyond words	22
Implications for teaching and learning	24
Further reading	24
Chapter 4 **Vocabulary size and growth**	25
The receptive vocabulary sizes of young native speakers of English	25
Testing the vocabulary size of young learners	29
Assessing productive vocabulary	33
Implications for teaching and learning	36
Further reading	37
Resources	37
Chapter 5 **Vocabulary and learning conditions**	38
Conditions supporting vocabulary learning	38
Receptive and productive use	39
Applying the learning conditions	41
Further reading	47
Chapter 6 **Oral language and vocabulary growth**	48
Talking and vocabulary learning	48
Gifting conversational exchanges	50
Other oral language sources	51
Multimedia oral language sources	54
Further reading	57
Chapter 7 **Vocabulary and reading**	58
Reading mileage	58
Guided or shared reading	59
A well-balanced reading programme	62
How children's books support vocabulary learning	65
Language use and language learning	68
Implications for teaching and learning	72
Further reading	73

Chapter 8 **Teaching vocabulary**	76
Vocabulary teaching techniques	79
Vocabulary learning exercises that require little or no preparation	81
Ensuring words are encountered many times	83
Providing vocabulary support for reading	84
Interference	85
Analysing deliberate learning activities	86
Implications for teaching and learning	94
Further reading	94
Chapter 9 **Word consciousness**	**96**
Word consciousness focus activities	97
Other word consciousness activities	118
Learning words	119
Implications for teaching and learning	120
Further reading	121
Resources	122
Chapter 10 **Helping learners with below-average vocabulary sizes**	**123**
Diagnosing vocabulary and reading problems	124
Guidelines for helping learners with below-average vocabulary sizes	124
Intensive reading	127
A balanced vocabulary development programme	128
Implications for teaching and learning	130
Further reading	131
Chapter 11 **Vocabulary learning procedures**	**132**
WordPlosion	132
Sharing vocabulary through group brainstorming	137
Word-focused rich instruction using high-frequency vocabulary	139
A final word	142
Appendices	143
Appendix 1 High-frequency, mid-frequency and low-frequency words	143
Appendix 2 The Picture Vocabulary Size Test	145
Appendix 3 Measuring vocabulary size: A yes/no test of the most frequent 24,000 words of English	149
Appendix 4 Guidelines for parents for helping with their child's reading and vocabulary growth	151
Appendix 5 A simple text marked for word frequency levels	155
Appendix 6 Steps in semantic mapping	157
Appendix 7 The most useful word stems	159
Appendix 8 The most useful prefixes and suffixes	164
Appendix 9 Steps for word experts	165
Appendix 10 A test of "What every primary teacher should know about vocabulary"	167
References	176
Bibliography	177
Index	180

Chapter 1 Introduction

Overview

This book is written for teachers of young children aged from 5 to 12 years in primary schools. Most of these children will be native speakers of English, although the increasing cultural and linguistic diversity of our communities suggests a significant number will be from homes where other languages are used dominantly or at least interwoven with English. 'Knowing your learners' should underpin teachers' pedagogical decisions and the pathways of learning followed in the classroom. When learners are not native speakers of English—in the strict sense of using English as the only or dominant language in the family—this needs to be taken account of in approaches to develop learners' vocabulary knowledge.

The book does not directly address learners' knowledge of other languages, but it is important to stress that not capitalising on each learner's language environments outside school is counterproductive. The book is focused on vocabulary learning for young school-age learners, and much of the book's content is relevant to the development of vocabulary knowledge of young learners in any language. There are sections that pertain specifically to English, but these sections may well suggest considering another language in the same light.

Useful resources that specifically consider non-native speakers of English are available, and are referenced at the end of this chapter. It is important to remember that knowing more than one language is an asset, and young learners deserve to carry forward their family's languages other than English. Vocabulary and language knowledge in other languages can and should be woven into mainstream classroom learning where English is the dominant or only language of instruction.

The book draws strongly on research, but it is written in a non-academic way so that teachers are given clear, direct advice on what to do about vocabulary. At the end of each chapter the most relevant and useful pieces of research are discussed so that teachers can read more deeply on particular topics and check that the research is being properly represented and applied.

This book contains many resources for teachers, such as a Picture Vocabulary Size Test, ready-to-use activities for word consciousness-raising and word learning, and information about word parts. There are also resources that can be used with the book when it is used in in-service workshops for teachers. These include, among other things, a frequency-marked text, a 50-item multiple-choice test on the ideas in the book, a vocabulary size measure, and the activities listed in column three of Table 1.1.

The book in a nutshell

Young native speakers of English and young second-language learners in an English-speaking environment will inevitably learn English. Young learners cannot avoid picking up the language around them. Even if teachers did nothing special about vocabulary learning, young children would increase their vocabulary knowledge. However, teachers can make vocabulary learning more effective, and this is particularly important for the vocabulary needed for schooling and academic learning.

Words are learned largely in relation to how often they are met (multiple meetings) and how deeply they are processed. Especially in the early years of a child's life, words are mainly learned through talk—hearing and trying out spoken language. Reading is also an important source of vocabulary learning, initially for young children through being read to accompanied by conversational talk, and later, as they become more independent readers, by reading widely on their own or with peers. Reading provides extra input and repetition, and allows learners to meet words not often used in spoken language.

Table 1.1 Topics and activities for an in-service course for teachers on vocabulary

	Topic	Activities
Chapter 2	The nature of vocabulary	• Apply the rule of thumb to working out the vocabulary size of learners of a given age (e.g. 10-year-olds). • Classify words into the high-, mid- and low- frequency levels. • Practise using the Frequency, Range and AntWordProfiler programs. • Look at frequency-marked texts to decide what words should be focused on for learners of a given age.
Chapter 3	Knowing vocabulary	• Choose a word and describe what could be known about its form, meaning and use, using Table 3.1 as a guide. • Suggest two activities in each of the four strands (a total of eight activities).
Chapter 4	Vocabulary size and growth	• Administer the Picture Vocabulary Size Test (PVST). • Sit the PVST yourself. • Sit the Vocabulary Size Test.
Chapter 5	Vocabulary and learning conditions	• Find examples of each of the conditions. • Analyse some activities using a checklist based on learning conditions. • Analyse an activity such as shared reading or a problem-solving task using the conditions.
Chapter 6	Oral language and vocabulary growth	• In pairs, demonstrate an elaborative conversation style with a learner about spiders.
Chapter 7	Vocabulary and reading	• Do the shared book activity. • Design a linked skills activity around a book. • Suggest two challenging language-use activities each for listening and for reading. • Suggest ways to increase the amount of reading your learners do. • Suggest ways to help learners deal with challenging reading.
Chapter 8	Teaching vocabulary	• Choose your top three vocabulary teaching activities and defend your choice. • State and explain the principle of the four strands. How does it apply to teaching vocabulary?
Chapter 9	Word consciousness	• Rank the focuses, considering their value for your learners. Be ready to justify your top three. • Do the activities in each section of that chapter.
Chapter 10	Helping learners with below-average vocabulary sizes	• Look at examples of text richness in spoken and written language use to see opportunities for learning.
Chapter 11	Vocabulary learning procedures	• Analyse some activities to see their parts.

The frequency and quality of talk exchanges or conversations a child is involved in is a major contributor to their learning of vocabulary. A second major oral language source is the increasingly wide range of digital material children have access to, especially through the internet. Usually the internet provides a combination of audio and visual, often accompanied by print, rather than audio only. Even very young children are likely to view and listen using digital sources.

An essential part of increasing young learners' vocabulary size is being engaged in plenty of reading. This may be through books, other non-digital sources, or through a myriad of texts now available digitally. When a child is young and an emerging reader, engaging in talk with an adult or older peer during reading is how they learn new words through print. As a child becomes increasingly able to read independently, many more words are available to them if they read often and widely. Ideally, young native speakers should be engaged in reading for at least an hour per school day, complemented by home reading, and participating often in high-quality spoken texts throughout the day.

Young native speakers of English increase their *receptive* vocabulary size (the vocabulary used for listening and reading) on average by around 500 to 1,000 words a year, or around two to three words per day. Some native speakers have smaller vocabulary increases but still learn several hundred words a year. Learners need to know at least 2,000 words for early reading (most 5-year-olds know at least 3,000 words), and around 6,000 words to cope with later reading in primary school.

Direct teaching of vocabulary can help a child learn new words. The focus should be on topic-related, context-relevant vocabulary. Chapter 11 describes powerful ways such words can be focused on as part of the classroom programme. To provide an extra boost in vocabulary growth of around 500 words a year beyond the normal increase, teachers may need to deliberately focus on vocabulary learning in the classroom. An exciting and effective way to do this is through developing *word consciousness*, whereby the learners are encouraged to become interested in words and are confident in ways of dealing with them.

Direct attention to vocabulary complements a strong focus on spoken language, reading, and rich language use in the classroom.

Specific vocabulary strategies—including breaking words into parts and doing *morphological problem-solving*, making use of dictionaries, talking about words, and deliberately studying words—will be further explained in later chapters.

What should teachers do?

1. Get learners consciously and actively engaged with words using a range of word consciousness activities and activities that enrich word meanings and focus on the use of words. An important goal is to get learners interested in and excited about vocabulary so that they initiate their own vocabulary learning as well as participating in focused discussion with others.

2. Focus on a rich conversational classroom in which learners have multiple opportunities to participate in spoken language that provides vocabulary the learners need, and that supports learners to try out newly available vocabulary.

3. Create a rich, extensive reading environment in the classroom to encourage learners to do large amounts of interesting and challenging reading, including reading for themselves and listening to and talking about books read to them.

4. During spoken and print-related activities, take the opportunity to explore and discuss the meanings of words.

5. Be systematic about helping learners expand their vocabulary size by making sure that each day there are planned opportunities (as in point 1 above) for vocabulary growth.

6. Gather continuous formative evidence about learners' vocabulary knowledge (their strengths and gaps) during class activities. This evidence is readily available when a conversational teaching and learning environment is created, where each learner gets plenty of opportunity to speak and respond. Use a suitable vocabulary size test to measure and track learners' overall vocabulary knowledge. We recommend the Picture Vocabulary Size Test.

7. Support learners in their writing to make effective word choices and stretch their word knowledge, and to use words that are appropriate to the topic, purpose and audience.

8. Learn more about the nature of vocabulary, including vocabulary size, vocabulary levels and the spread of word frequency, what is involved in knowing a word, and the conditions that support vocabulary learning across the four strands (discussed later).

Chapter 2 The nature of vocabulary

The most striking feature of vocabulary is that words are used with different frequencies, and this fact has a strong effect on which vocabulary teachers should focus on, how vocabulary is learned, and how it should be taught.

Basic ideas

In order to do research on vocabulary, frequency information about words is gathered from large collections of texts and is used to arrange words into groups of 1,000 words, with the most frequent 1,000 words put into the first 1,000 words, the second most frequent 1,000 words put into the second 1,000 words and so on. These lists of words and programs to use them are available from Paul Nation's website (http://www.victoria.ac.nz/lals/staff/paul-nation.aspx). These lists have been used for analysing the vocabulary load of texts, investigating opportunities to learn vocabulary, and making vocabulary size tests.

We can use these lists to divide words into high-frequency, mid-frequency and-low frequency words. By the time young native speakers start school they already know most of the 3,000 high-frequency words, if they have had a stimulating and varied language environment. 'Knowing' may range from receptive knowledge for most words (meeting in spoken language and reading), and productive knowledge (used in speaking or writing) for many but not all. By the time native speakers begin secondary school they are very likely to know all or most of the 3,000 high-frequency words and most of the 6,000 mid-frequency words, totalling 9,000 words. They will also know some of the low-frequency words.

Most words are learned in rough order of the frequency they are used across a wide range of texts. For example, the highest frequency words are ones that occur over and over in oral and written English texts—words such as *the, I, then, often, mother, take, talk*. Mid-frequency words are used less often but often enough to be words an English speaker and reader needs to know to handle a range of texts in English—words such as *calf, cupboard, doom, giggle, pest, precaution*. Low-frequency words occur much less often during everyday language use. Low frequency words include words that you are unlikely to encounter again in a short time unless there is a specific topic in focus—*skylark, marsupial, excrete, haze, bristle, hydrofoil, vitreous*. Learners tend to learn high-frequency and mid-frequency words before they begin learning large quantities of low-frequency words. However, low-frequency words arise in many contexts in which young native speakers might be involved, so they have the potential to learn these low-frequency words in context.

Because many mid-frequency words do not occur very frequently, learners need to meet words through large amounts of spoken language and reading in order to have a good chance of learning them. This learning can be increased if the learners give attention to these words in effective ways.

Words can be grouped into *families*, where all the members of a family share the same word stem and have similar meanings. The members differ from each other largely as a result of the prefixes or suffixes they contain. Being able to see these relationships is a very important way in which learners increase the number of words they know.

Vocabulary size and word frequency

When you focus on words in class, check out that the words are useful for the learners by being at the word frequency level the learners can cope with. How can you do this? First, estimate the vocabulary size of your learners. A simple way to estimate this for the average learner to is to take their age, subtract 2, and multiply by 1,000. This means that an 8-year-old is likely know around 6,000 words (8 minus 2 = 6, times 1,000 = 6,000). To check more precisely, young learners can be given the Picture Vocabulary Size Test, which measures young learners' vocabulary size up to the sixth 1,000 words. The most frequent 6,000 words of English is a list of words from the most frequent to the least frequent. This list was broken into 12 frequency-ranked groups of 500 words and these 12 lists were used to provide words for the test.

Secondly, develop a feeling for what the mid-frequency words of English are. This feel for what words to pay attention to for particular learners can be termed 'working in their Goldilocks zone'. It means being aware of words that learners have the potential to learn: not too simple, not too hard; not too many, not too few; not too fast, not too slowly; not too often, not too infrequently. Just right!

Appendix 1 of this book contains an exercise that will give you some practice in recognising various word levels. If a word is a mid-frequency word, it is useful to focus on it.

Table 2.1 shows how different vocabulary levels apply to different age levels in a school. It is a broad generalisation from data gathered by Biemiller and colleagues in Canada (Biemiller & Slonim, 2001, Bielmiller, 2005), and from using the Picture Vocabulary Size Test and the Vocabulary Size Test in New Zealand schools. Ages do vary at various school years, and the vocabulary size ranges do not include a few individual extremes.

Table 2.1 Age, school year and vocabulary sizes

Age	School year	Vocabulary size range	Levels to focus on
5	1	2,500–3,500 words	Mid-frequency (3,000 on)
6	2	3,000–4,500 words	Mid-frequency (4,000 on)
7	3	4,000–5,500 words	Mid-frequency (5,000 on)
8	4	5,000–6,500 words	Mid-frequency (6,000 on)
9	5	6,000–7,500 words	Mid-frequency
10	6	7,000–8,500 words	Mid-frequency
11	7	8,000–9,500 words	Low frequency
12	8	9,000–10,500 words	Low frequency

Using word frequencies

Word frequency lists

One way of looking at frequency is to turn a text into a frequency list. This involves listing every different word in the text and counting how often each one occurs. Fortunately there are computer programs that can quickly do this for us.

Table 2.2 is a frequency count of one of Grimm's Fairy Tales, *The Travelling Musicians*. The story is 1,371 words long and contains 466 different word forms. Table 2.2 shows the number of words occurring at various frequency levels.

Table 2.2 A word frequency count of *The Travelling Musicians*

Freq	No. of words	Freq	No. of words	Freq	No. of words	Freq	No. of words
115	1	19	1	12	2	6	4
60	1	18	2	11	3	5	11
40	1	16	2	10	6	4	26
38	1	15	2	9	1	3	30
26	1	14	3	8	6	2	61
20	1	13	1	7	5	1	293

Table 2.2 shows that one word (*the*) occurred 115 times, six words occurred 10 times in the story, and 293 words occurred only once. Note the following two points.

- Well over half of the different words in the story (293 out of 466) occur only once. That is, most of the words in the story are not repeated. Here are some of the words occurring only once: *stabbed, roadside, robber, mice, livelihood*.
- A small number of words occur very frequently and make up a very large proportion of the story. If we add up the frequency figures for the words in the first two columns, multiplying them by the number of words with that frequency, the 17 different words total 458 running words (almost 35% of the running words in the story). When we count *running words*, we simply count every word that occurs and if the same word occurs four times for example, it is counted as four running words. The most frequent word, occurring 115 times, is *the*; the second most frequent word, occurring 60 times, is *and*; and the third most frequent, occurring 40 times, is *a*.

What are the implications of these two points? First, a lot of the different words in a text occur very infrequently, and in order to learn these words learners need to meet words through large amounts of spoken language and reading. The words need to be encountered so that the learners have a high chance of grasping the word's meaning in context. These words can make reading a text with fullness of meaning difficult if they are not understood. Some learners, such as learners from language backgrounds other than English, may need carefully selected reading texts that provide vocabulary in their Goldilocks zone, and in a manner that offers them the potential to understand and learn these words.

Second, there are some very common words that need to be learned before moving on to less generally useful words. Not all words are created equal, and useful words need to be learned before less useful words. This is not to suggest that incidental learning of less frequently occurring words (low-frequency vocabulary) is not useful and does not occur. Even very young children can be fascinated with some words they hear, and they learn these well before the time we would expect them to be learned. Dinosaur names are a striking example. Young native speakers, before they begin reading, already know several thousand words they have learned through listening and speaking.

Word families

Table 2.3 shows the results of another way of analysing the vocabulary of the story. This time the words in the story were classified according to their frequency level in the language as a whole. The classification is done by using lists of word families that have been compiled by using data from very large collections of texts. Each word list used in the analysis in Table 2.3 contains 1,000 word families, and there are 25 lists, making a total of 25,000 word families.[1] Instead of counting individual word forms, they count related words as being in the same family. When we talk about 'words' in this book, we are usually referring to word families, unless otherwise noted. Here are two examples of families from the lists.

---

1   They are available free from Paul Nation's website and are called the BNC/COCA lists. See also http://www.lextutor.ca/vp/kids/ for a text analysis program.

Table 2.3 Two examples of word families

accept	act
acceptability	acted
acceptable	acting
acceptably	action
acceptance	actionable
acceptances	actioned
accepted	actioning
accepting	actions
acceptor	actor
acceptors	actors
accepts	actress
unacceptability	actresses
unacceptable	acts
unacceptably	inaction
	unactioned

The two examples in Table 2.3 are quite big families, and some of the members of these families are very uncommon. All the members of a family have a close form and meaning relationship to the head word of the family and to other members. Some families, however, such as *across*, *the*, *alone* and *at*, have only a single word in the family.

In general, the more frequent a family, the more members it is likely to have, even though many of these members will not be very frequent. We group words into families for the purposes of reading and listening. Knowing one or two members of a family and being familiar with the common word-building prefixes and suffixes make it relatively easy to understand other members of the family. 'Knowing' in this case, means understanding the word's underlying meaning. Knowing the underlying meaning of the head word makes it easier to learn other members in the word family and to work out their meaning in a variety of contexts. Having such word family lists makes it easier—and certainly much more systematic—to decide in what order to teach and learn words and to analyse the vocabulary load of texts.

Table 2.4 Word family frequency level analysis of *The Travelling Musicians*

Word family frequency level	Coverage of text	Cumulative coverage
1st 1,000	88.48%	(1,000+ others) 88.99%
2nd 1,000	3.87%	92.86%
3rd 1,000	0.80%	93.66%
4th to 9th 1,000s	5.69%	99.50%
10th 1,000 on	0.65%	100.00%
Others	0.51%	
Total	100%	

Column 3 in Table 2.4 shows that for this text the most frequent 1,000 word families of English (88.48%) plus "others" (0.51%) (proper nouns, exclamations and transparent compounds) cover 88.99% of the text. The first 3,000 word families of English (which we call the high-frequency words) cover 93.66% of the running words in the text. The next 6,000 word families (the fourth to ninth 1,000s) cover 5.69%. These are called the mid-frequency words of English. The remaining word families (the low-frequency words), which include the 10th 1,000 and all the 1,000 word levels after that, cover 0.65% of the running words.

Here are some words from the text from each of the high-, mid- and low-frequency levels:

- high frequency: *the, he, master, one, sleep, journey, pray, concert, monster, eager*
- mid-frequency: *march, ass, donkey, grope, horrid, scamper*
- low frequency: *abode, rascal, hobgoblin.*

The kind of analysis done in Table 2.4 shows how knowledge of the language (particularly its vocabulary) can affect the difficulty of a text. If a learner knew only the first 1,000 word families of English, they would know a lot of the running words in the text (88.48% or 88.99%, if we accept that the 'others' are words that do not need to be known before reading the text). This is roughly eight out of every nine running words. However, knowing the first 1,000 word families would still not be enough to read the text comfortably and with fullness of meaning, because 11.1% of the running words (one word out of every nine) would be an unknown word. That is the equivalent of one unknown word in every single 10-word line of the text. Let's see what that would look like.

Box 2.1 A text marked to show the effect of not knowing low-frequency words

The Travelling Musicians

An honest farmer had once an YYYY that had been a YYYY servant to him a great many years, but was now growing old and every day more and more unfit for work. His master YYYY was tired of keeping him and began to think of putting an end to him; but the YYYY, who saw that some YYYY was in the wind, took himself YYYY off, and began his YYYY towards the great city, 'for there,' thought he, 'I may become a musician.'

After he had travelled a little way, he YYYY a dog lying by the roadside and YYYY as if he were tired. 'What makes you YYYY so, my friend?' said the YYYY. 'YYYY!' said the dog, 'My master was going to knock me on the head, because I am old and YYYY, and can no longer make myself useful to him in hunting; so I ran away; but what can I do to YYYY my YYYY?'

In the text, all the words not replaced by YYYY are in the first 1,000 words of English (see Chapter 7 for the complete text). This shows how important the high-frequency words are, and how not knowing the lower-frequency words can make learners struggle to read the text.

The division of word families into high frequency, mid-frequency and low frequency is largely based on the coverage of text. In general, the 3,000 high-frequency words cover around 95% of the running words in a text that young learners are likely to encounter. Adding the 6,000 mid-frequency words results in a coverage of around 98% of most texts. The low-frequency words account for the remaining 2%. If we exclude proper nouns, transparent compound words where the meaning of a word's parts are clearly related to the meaning of the whole word, for example, *snowball*, *bathroom*, and marginal words like *gosh*, *gee*, *um*, and *er*, there are probably well over 30,000 to 40,000 low-frequency word families, many of which will be technical words. This figure is not much more than an educated guess because we do not yet have lists of word families much beyond the 25,000 level. A large number of the words that are not high- or mid-frequency words are proper nouns or very technical, specialised words.

Table 2.5 The three frequency levels of vocabulary

Level	No. of words	Cumulative number	Cumulative text coverage*
High frequency	3,000	3,000	95%
Mid-frequency	6,000	9,000	98%
Low frequency	30,000	39,000	100%

* This coverage includes proper nouns, transparent compounds, marginal words and acronyms.

Instead of using frequency, there are other ways of dividing words into groups. An important way is to group words according to their relevance to a particular text, to a group of texts on the same topic or in the same area of specialisation, or to a whole genre of texts.

Subject matter vocabulary

Each text has its own topic-related vocabulary. The problem with focusing on this vocabulary is that it is unlikely to help much with reading tomorrow's text. However, if learners are working on a series of related texts, this overcomes the problem. There is likely to be a special vocabulary for children's stories, a special vocabulary for social studies, and so on. Here are some words that are not usually in the high-frequency words of English but that occur quite a lot in children's stories.

Box 2.2 Words likely to appear in stories for children

cat	monkey	fox	spider	king
dog	elephant	duck	sparrow	fairy
horse	snake	worm	goat	dragon
pony	lion	rooster	butterfly	prince
cow	zebra	tortoise	bull	princess
fish	giraffe	zebra	hen	witch
bird	crocodile	kitten	hare	magic
insect	wolf	crab	parrot	spell
fly	mouse	whale	lizard	monster
moth	frog	donkey	crow	palace
caterpillar	lamb	hedgehog		noble
earwig	pig	squirrel		treasure
				majesty

Vocabulary goals

What words and how many words do learners need to know? We will look at these two questions in much more detail in later chapters. The high-frequency vocabulary is essential knowledge, and by the time first-language learners enter school at the age of 5 or 6 they will already know many or most of these words orally. By the time they enter secondary school, around the age of 13, they will also know most of the mid-frequency vocabulary. For various reasons—largely related to hobbies, interests and opportunities—they will also know several or even many hundred other words in the low-frequency range. These may include, for example, the names of dinosaurs, words related to computing and games, words learned from their favourite stories and their areas of interest, alongside low-frequency words they meet in their daily life.

There are many estimates of the number of words that learners need to know, and they differ by very large amounts. There are two major reasons for these differences. First, often different things are being counted. Some researchers count different word forms, so that *boy*, *boys* and *boy's* are counted as three different words (technically called word types). Some count inflected forms as belonging to the same word (this is called counting lemmas), so that *boy*, *boys* and *boy's* would be counted as the same word or lemma, but *boyish* and *boyhood* would each be a different lemma, because they are distinctly 'different' words even though they belong to the same word family. Some count both inflected and clearly related derived forms as belonging to the same word family (this is the approach taken in this book). This means that *boy*, *boys*, *boy's*, *boyish* and *boyhood* are counted as belonging to the same family. Counting word types results in many more words than counting lemmas or word families. Some researchers count proper nouns (the names of people and places, usually written with a capital letter) as included in the lists of words needing to be learned, while others exclude them on the grounds that they need not be known before reading a text. These differences in the unit used for counting and what is considered as a word can have very striking effects on the number of words included in a vocabulary goal.

A second reason for the variation in vocabulary sizes is that some counts are methodologically wrong, often because they have not clearly defined the unit of counting and have wrongly estimated the size of their corpus or the dictionary they are using.

It is useful to know in general how many words young native speakers know because teachers tend to underestimate the vocabulary size of their learners and the rate of their vocabulary growth. It is also important to realise that words differ greatly in their usefulness for learners of different ages. Vocabulary learning is continuous and largely systematic, and teaching needs to take account of this. In the following chapters we will look at what it means to know a word, vocabulary size and growth, and how words are learned.

Further reading

To find out the rules for making word families, see:

L. Bauer, & I. S. P. Nation. (1993). Word families. *International Journal of Lexicography*, 6(4), 253–279.

Resources

To get a free frequency counting program, download a version of the Range program from Paul Nation's website (http://www.victoria.ac.nz/lals/staff/paul-nation.aspx). A copy of the program Frequency.exe is included in the download. This program processes plain text files and is very easy to use. To make a plain text file from a Word document, open the Word file, go to the File menu and choose *Save as*. Click the down arrow in the *Save as type* box at the bottom of the dialogue box, and choose *Plain text*. You can find a web-based frequency program at http://www.lextutor.ca. A useful profiler tool available to analyse young learner texts on this site is: http://www.lextutor.ca/vp/kids/. See Appendix 5 for an example analysis of a simple text.

To get a free word frequency levels program, go to Laurence Anthony's website (http://www.antlab.sci.waseda.ac.jp/antwordprofiler_index.html) and download AntWordProfiler.

Chapter 3 Knowing vocabulary

In Chapter 2 we looked at what words learners need to know and how many words they need. But what does it mean to *know* a word? This chapter describes the kinds of knowledge that learners have when they truly know a word. The title of this chapter is *Knowing vocabulary*, because, as we shall see, knowing words is only a part of knowing vocabulary. So another goal of this chapter is provide a broad view of what is involved in knowing vocabulary. Finally, we look briefly at how learners can develop their knowledge of vocabulary. Learning vocabulary will be dealt with in more detail in later chapters.

Knowing a word

When we say that we 'know' a word, this usually means we can recognise this word when we hear or see it and can give a meaning for it. This is one of the most useful kinds of word knowledge, but, as Table 3.1 shows, there is much more to knowing a word.

Table 3.1 is divided into three major sections: form, meaning and use. Each of these sections is also divided into three. So the section on form includes knowledge of the spoken form of a word, knowledge of the written form, and knowledge of word parts (i.e. prefixes, stems and suffixes). Note that each type of knowledge is divided into two parts: receptive and productive. So, knowledge of spoken form can be receptive (we can recognise the word when we hear it), or productive (we can say and use the word when we need it to express a meaning).

Table 3.1 What is involved in knowing a word?

Form	spoken	R	What does the word sound like?
		P	How is the word pronounced?
	written	R	What does the word look like?
		P	How is the word written and spelled?
	word parts	R	What parts are recognisable in this word?
		P	What word parts are needed to express the meaning?
Meaning	form and meaning	R	What meaning does this word form signal?
		P	What word form can be used to express this meaning?
	concept and referents	R	What is included in the concept?
		P	What items can the concept refer to?
	associations	R	What other words does this make us think of?
		P	What other words could we use instead of this one?
Use	grammatical functions	R	In what patterns does the word occur?
		P	In what patterns must we use this word?
	collocations	R	What words or types of words occur with this one?
		P	What words or types of words must we use with this one?
	constraints on use	R	Where, when, and how often would we expect to meet this word?
		P	Where, when, and how often can we use this word?

Source: Nation, 2013a

Key: R = receptive knowledge, P = productive knowledge.

The various aspects of knowledge shown in Table 3.1 do not all need to be taught. They are developed in a variety of ways. The most common way is to learn them in meaningful contexts through meeting and using words in spoken and written language. It is likely that at least the 9,000 high-frequency and mid-frequency word families are largely learned through listening and speaking. This may be supported by wide and varied reading. Even native speakers who cannot read well know most of these words by the time they begin secondary school at the age of around 13. Reading certainly helps with vocabulary learning because it provides experience with the written form, increases the number of encounters with the words, puts the words in new contexts, and develops a richer knowledge of the world and concepts that support vocabulary knowledge. Written text also uses a much richer vocabulary than most spoken text, and is especially helpful in developing knowledge of low-frequency words.

Some aspects of word knowledge are also developed through deliberate attention—through looking words up in the dictionary, through having them explained in context, through being taught about them, occasionally through deliberate memorisation, through word part analysis, and through deliberately noticing new uses and forms. Paying explicit attention to words arising in texts in the classroom is a good way of increasing learners' vocabulary knowledge, especially for learning across the curriculum.

Some aspects of knowledge are developed through our everyday experience of the world. For example, if I tell you the meaning of a word you have probably not met before, you are likely to be able to tell me some possible collocations of the word, and its possible associates and whether it is likely to be a frequently used word or not. Here is an example: "*ferronière* = jewel on a chain that hangs in the centre of your forehead". Try answering these questions. What adjectives could go with this word? Who is likely to wear a *ferronière*? Can you use this word in a sentence? This presumes knowledge of the syntax or structure of language, which is likely to be strongly in place for native speakers of a language.

Some aspects of knowledge are part of the language system, and once we have a basic level of proficiency we can predict how the system applies to words we have just met. Let's use the example of *ferronière* again. Do you think this word can also have a plural form? How would you pronounce this word? Where is the stress in the word? If you only heard the word, could you roughly spell it?

The reason for looking at these different ways in which our knowledge of words develops is to show that teaching makes up only a small part of how we develop our knowledge of vocabulary. Most vocabulary learning occurs without teaching. When we consider how many thousands of words learners need to know, we can see that teaching could only account for a very small part of the vocabulary learning needed.

The number one requirement for vocabulary learning is large amounts of language input at the right level for the learners. This means lots of interesting and relevant spoken language and reading.

This is such an important requirement that a teacher's main concern regarding vocabulary should be: are my learners involved in supportive, participatory talk and other oral language opportunities, and reading?

The number two requirement for vocabulary learning in school should be that the learners are supported and extended in their encounters and use of new and partly known vocabulary. This can occur through effective learning talk and reading in the classroom. It can also occur though activities such as linked skills tasks, and the chance to apply and re-apply content knowledge that has been recently learned. It is especially helpful when learners engage in learning talk and there is reading in abundance throughout a school day. Activities involving words recently learned also offer learners extended opportunities to enrich their word knowledge.

The number three requirement is that the teacher should give deliberate repeated attention to words that are closely related to the subject areas the learners are studying, including explanation of words in context. Some of this vocabulary will be words that are beyond their present level of vocabulary knowledge. Ideally, this vocabulary teaching should be done as part of the content learning of the subject area and not as decontextualised vocabulary teaching. When the vocabulary teaching is done as pre-teaching before reading, it should be linked to the text to come in some way, and talked about in ways such that the learners realise that the pre-reading words are important to know before reading the text. Where possible, the teaching should draw on the strategies described in the number four requirement.

The number four requirement is that learners are supported to develop positive attitudes to words, particularly through conscious applied vocabulary learning strategies. These include, in decreasing order of importance:

- noticing and being attentive to words (word consciousness)
- a willingness to ask what words mean
- dictionary use (including electronic dictionaries)
- word part analysis (including deliberately learning useful prefixes, suffixes and word stems)
- some practice in guessing from context
- the application of a few basic spelling rules.

An important goal of strategy development is to get learners excited about vocabulary and consciously aware of words and their nature. A useful way of helping to do this is to get learners to become *word experts*. This involves learners being excited by words, noticing them, independently researching particular words, and reporting on their findings to their classmates (see Appendix 9 for guidelines).

The very important message of the first part of this chapter is that vocabulary learning occurs largely through meaning-focused input, and it is very important that learners get plenty of input that is suited to their level of knowledge and stretches their knowledge and vocabulary. This input occurs through meaningfully engaging in quality spoken language, and through reading.

Beyond words

In the strategy described above, we looked beyond single words to encompass more system-related features of vocabulary. Knowing vocabulary includes not only knowing words, but also knowing how to use them, knowing how to analyse them, knowing the systems they fit into, knowing something about their history, recognising when they are used well or not, and when they are used in ways that may not be obvious.

Language learning in general, and vocabulary learning in particular, benefits from having four kinds of opportunities for learning:

- learning through meaning-focused input (someone else's language available and noticed by the learner)
- learning through meaning-focused output (trying out using language—oral or written)
- learning through language-focused learning
- learning through fluency development.

These opportunities are called the *four strands*, because they should run through teaching and learning approaches and contexts as four long, continuous strands.

There are some vocabulary-related systems that native speakers use without being aware of them. These include recognising and producing the spoken forms of words, using words in a range of different related senses, using prefixes and suffixes (such as plural *-s*, *-ly* for adverbs, and *un-*), and using words with the right accompanying words (collocation). Knowledge of these systems develops through incidental learning and is more likely when language use by and with the learner is rich and frequent.

There are other vocabulary-related systems that require some conscious learning, and these include developing sight vocabulary for reading, developing knowledge of phonics (how spoken use of a language is recorded in written form), learning to spell, and seeing connections between words containing the same word stems—head word derivatives.

The systems that are learned incidentally require plenty of spoken and written input at the right level for the learner. The systems that require conscious learning require learning across the four strands. Conscious learning occurs largely in the language-focused learning strand, and it is important that this learning is supported by opportunities to learn through the other three strands. For example, learning useful word parts can begin as a deliberate learning activity, but the word parts learned in this way need to be met again in reading and spoken language, sometimes in combinations that were not deliberately studied. The prefix *pre-*, meaning 'before', for example, can be deliberately learned, and this learning is strengthened when it is met again in reading or spoken language in words such as *pre-school* and *premature*. Knowledge is strengthened when it is produced in some words. Having to produce language features in message-focused communication helps turn receptive knowledge into productive knowledge.

In this chapter we have looked at what it means to 'know' a word and how this knowledge is gained. Although knowing a word involves a lot of aspects of knowledge, this knowledge is largely developed through opportunities for receptive use (listening and reading) and productive use (speaking and writing). Direct teaching of vocabulary has a role to play, but it is a limited role. Teachers need to direct most of their efforts towards making sure that learners are getting plenty of opportunities for meaning-focused language use, and that this language use is setting up good conditions for language learning. Developing a strong word-conscious environment in the classroom will contribute significantly to developing individual learners' noticing and attention to partially known and new vocabulary. Their vocabulary growth will be influenced most strongly by the quantity and quality of the language use available to them in both input and output.

Implications for teaching and learning

1. Most vocabulary learning occurs incidentally, through engagement with spoken language and reading. This includes not only learning new words but strengthening and enriching partly known words.

2. Teaching can only account for a small proportion of vocabulary learning, and it should be directed towards subject-matter-related vocabulary, and towards developing the strategies of dictionary use, word part analysis, guessing from context, and a few spelling rules. A word-learning attitude needs to be *taught* and *caught* in the classroom. Being excited about words—sharing known and new words as they arise—ignites word learning. A core role a teacher needs to play is to provide opportunities and rich contexts whereby vocabulary within the learner's Goldilocks zone is frequently and meaningfully available.

3. The strategy of word part analysis might best begin when learners are around 7 or 8 years old, and focusing initially on the most useful prefixes and stems, and expanding on this knowledge over time.

Further reading

Table 3.1 is taken from Chapter 2 of:

I. S. P. Nation. (2013). *Learning vocabulary in another language.* (2nd ed.). Cambridge, UK: Cambridge University Press.

For more on the four strands, see:

I. S. P. Nation. (2007). The four strands. *Innovation in Language Learning and Teaching*, *1*(1), 1–12.

This is available free under **Publications** on Paul Nation's website (http://www.victoria.ac.nz/lals/staff/paul-nation.aspx)

Chapter 4 Vocabulary size and growth

In Chapter 2 we looked at the nature of vocabulary and how we can distinguish three levels of high-frequency, mid-frequency and low-frequency words. We also saw that there are large numbers of words to learn. In Chapter 3 we looked at what is involved in knowing a word and how this knowledge can be developed. In this chapter we look at how much vocabulary young native speakers of English are likely to know. Are they likely to know enough words to understand what they read and hear, speak and write, without vocabulary being a major problem? We also look at how we can measure how much vocabulary our learners know.

The receptive vocabulary sizes of young native speakers of English

In Chapter 2 we looked at receptive and productive vocabulary. In this chapter we focus on receptive vocabulary knowledge—the kind of knowledge needed for comprehending what someone else is saying and reading.

In Chapter 2 we looked at the very rough rule of thumb for how many word families an average young native speaker knows, namely take the learner's age, subtract 2, and multiply the result by 1,000. This means that a 6-year-old knows around 4,000 word families (6 − 2 x 1,000 = 4,000). An 8-year-old knows around 6,000 word families. This rough rule of thumb seems to work up to the age of about 17 or 18 years.

The small amount of research on young native speakers' vocabulary size generally supports this rule of thumb (Biemiller, 2005; Biemiller

& Slonim, 2001). The test used by Biemiller was a fairly tough test, where each learner was asked to say what they knew about a particular word. The researchers did not expect to get perfect definitions or explanations from children aged from 5 to 11 years old and scored a word as known if the learner provided some relevant information about the word. Table 4.1 gives rounded figures for the vocabulary sizes of young children according to Biemiller.

Table 4.1 Average native speaker vocabulary sizes for various age levels

Age	Average vocabulary size	Range of sizes
5 years	3,000 word families	1,000–5,000
6 years	4,000 word families	1,500–5,000
7 years	5,000 word families	2,000–8,500
8 years	6,000 word families	3,000–10,000
9 years	7,000 word families	4,000–11,000
10 years	8,000 word families	5,500–12,000
11 years	9,000 word families	7,000–13,000

Each year we would expect a vocabulary size increase of just under 1,000 word families for children getting adequate amounts of oral and written language. Research shows, however, that at any age or school year level there is quite a large variation in vocabulary size between different individuals. Biemiller's figures fit well with our own research in New Zealand secondary schools, where, on average, 13-year-olds knew around 10,500 word families with ranges from 7,000 to 17,000. Only a very small number of those tested scored at these extremes.

There are several points to note about these figures.

- Even those with smallest vocabulary sizes know a lot of word families, unless they are new learners of English.
- Learners who know fewer words than the average at the age of 6 years probably know fewer words at the age of 13, and so on. This does not apply to children who are new learners of English who are making good progress in learning the language. They can often have strong vocabulary growth spurts, especially when their own language is closely related to English.

- The differences in vocabulary knowledge are likely to be more readily addressed when children are younger. This is because the actual number of unknown words involved at their level of proficiency is much fewer. The higher the frequency of the unknown words, the greater the chance they have of being learnt through more intensive language use. Learning is affected by the quality and quantity of conversations, reading and listening opportunities, and writing and talking.
- Additional vocabulary increases would need to be at least 500 words per year for the lower vocabulary size learners. This works out at around 12 words per week for 40 school weeks, or about three words per school day. Note that this is in addition to normal vocabulary growth.

Our findings from vocabulary testing using the Picture Vocabulary Size Test in New Zealand primary schools also largely agree with Biemiller's findings, even though we used a different test from him. We found that 6-year-olds knew 3,500 to 4,000 words, and 8-year-olds 4,500 to 5,000 words, with low-decile learners on average about 500 words behind high-decile learners.

Young native speakers seem to increase their vocabulary roughly according to frequency of occurrence; that is, the number of times they meet the words. Using word frequency levels we can roughly predict the words they need to learn next. However, frequency is by no means a perfect predictor, because the frequency lists that are available are typically not based on the kinds of language that young children use and meet. In addition, children are interested in unusual things, and so low-frequency words like *brontosaurus, witch, alligator, sleigh* and *ladybug* tend to be well known, although several of these occur well beyond the 10th 1,000 word level in frequency lists. Nonetheless, as young native speakers' vocabulary size increases, they usually fill in gaps in their knowledge of the high-frequency words and gaps in their knowledge of the early levels of the mid-frequency words. The more they read and engage with high-quality oral language texts, the more likely gaps are to be filled and vocabulary growth occurs.

Vocabulary researchers and reading researchers are generally concerned about the differences in vocabulary size between learners of the same age level. Some young native speakers have vocabulary sizes that are 2,000 or more word families smaller than others of the same age with an average vocabulary size. If we see vocabulary size as increasing at around 500 to 1,000 word families a year, this is the equivalent of being 1 to 2 years behind in vocabulary growth. There are many pieces of research that show this vocabulary gap between native speakers of different socioeconomic levels. See van Hees (2011) for a New Zealand example and Farkas and Berron (2004) for an example from the United States. Typically, lower socio-economic learners lag around 2 years behind higher socio-economic learners.

It is no simple matter to untangle the cause–effect relationships between vocabulary size, language use, life experience and a variety of other factors. However, it is probably safe to say that any 'catch up' intervention aimed at increasing vocabulary knowledge and improving language use should involve:

- increasing the amount of challenging, task-focused oral interactions and conversations, and oral language use opportunities
- increasing the amount of reading that learners do
- increasing the number of scaffolded and independent writing opportunities
- carrying out carefully focused, regular, deliberate vocabulary learning and teaching
- providing training in strategies for vocabulary growth and improved language use
- providing a great deal of language use across the four skills of listening, speaking, reading and writing to include language that is just beyond learners' current knowledge.

These actions would be facilitated if the learners know the purposes of each action to support their growth in vocabulary knowledge, and if they have a clear idea of their roles in helping them open up pathways to learning success. For example, learners need to know that trying to recall words (retrieval) helps learning and is more effective than just looking at words and their meanings. Similarly, noting words for later deliberate attention can make learning more certain. Where these actions are primarily school-based, closely relating them to school topics and curriculum areas is helpful.

Rather than seeing vocabulary growth as an attempt to bring lower percentile learners closer to the mean (which would then change the position of the mean), it may be better to determine the minimum vocabulary sizes needed to cope with texts at various year levels or groupings of year levels, and aim for these. This would then provide a clear, stable target rather than a shifting target.

It is important to at least narrow the vocabulary gap, even if catch-up and keep-up prove too challenging. Fortunately, as a learner's vocabulary size increases, the effect of a gap of the same size decreases. This is because a gap made up of low-frequency words has less effect on the vocabulary coverage of texts than a gap made up of high-frequency words. Learners with larger vocabulary sizes are likely to increase their vocabulary knowledge at a faster rate than learners with smaller vocabulary sizes. The rich will tend to get richer, but teachers need to make sure that at least the poor do not get poorer. Research by Farkas and Beron (2004) shows that the vocabulary size gap between high and low socioeconomic learners is established by about the age of 5 and is persistent unless there is a determined effort to support a very rapid gain of vocabulary knowledge for learners who have lower levels of vocabulary knowledge at an early schooling age.

What is clearly demonstrated when working with primary school learners—whether younger or older—is their amazing capacity to learn new words. Vocabulary in the learners' Goldilocks zone often becomes learned and used quickly. Teachers should set realistic but high goals, knowing that learners are very capable of learning when engaged in meaningful language use.

Testing the vocabulary size of young learners

One of the big gaps in the tools available to teachers and researchers is a reliable test of vocabulary size that can be used with young learners, many of whom are just beginning to learn to read. Each testing format has its advantages and disadvantages, but as long as test users are aware of these it is possible to design useful tests.

Interview tests

One way of testing young learners is to ask them individually what each word means. Usually each word is presented in a sentence to direct the learners towards a certain meaning or sense and to make the test a little like normal language use. If the learner can give some kind of relevant meaning or partial meaning for the word, the word is scored as known. The disadvantages of this format are that it is time-consuming (each learner needs to be tested individually), it is quite a demanding test (the learner has to recall the meaning rather than recognise it in a set of choices), and younger learners have difficulty defining words they obviously know. In addition, different testers may have different ideas about whether an answer is acceptable.

The advantages of this format are that learners do not have to be able to read in order to do the test, the test items are very easy to make, guessing plays virtually no part in answering, testers can press for a little more information and can take gestures and pointing into account as answers (such as a learner pointing at their face to show what *face* means), and the tester can keep the learners on task and motivated to do the test well by giving them encouraging feedback. Biemiller and Slonim (2001) used this format in their testing of young native speakers, and White, Graves and Slater (1990) used a similar test.

Multiple-choice or matching picture vocabulary tests

Picture vocabulary tests involve the learner hearing a word or a word in a sentence context and then having to point at one of several pictures to show the meaning of the word (see Figure 4.1). The disadvantages of this format are that these tests are difficult to make, some words are not readily tested through pictures, and random guessing can play a role in answering. The advantages are that no reading is required, scoring is reliable and easy, the test can be administered and scored on a computer, learners can easily show that they have some knowledge of a word, and testing can be done fairly quickly. The most well-known test of this type is the Peabody Picture Vocabulary Test. This test does not give a measure of total vocabulary size, but it is very useful for comparing against norms and between learners.

A different test, the Picture Vocabulary Size Test, was specially developed to measure the vocabulary size of pre-literate learners. It measures vocabulary knowledge up to the sixth 1,000 word families, and thus can be used with native speakers up to the age of 8 years, or non-native speakers who have been learning and using English for at least 3 or 4 years. Some children starting school at 5 years of age who were born in New Zealand, may fall into the second group because at home their families dominantly use a language or languages other than English. In the test, the learners listen to a short sentence, which also appears in written form, and then choose the picture that best illustrates it from a choice of four pictures.

The tested words have been chosen from a set of twelve 500-word lists that were created from a corpus of largely spoken texts, plus *School Journal*s and books for beginning readers. The lists thus contain vocabulary that young learners of English are most likely to know. Each learner's score on the test is converted to an estimate of the number of words they know from those 6,000 words.

Figure 4.1 The Picture Vocabulary Size Test

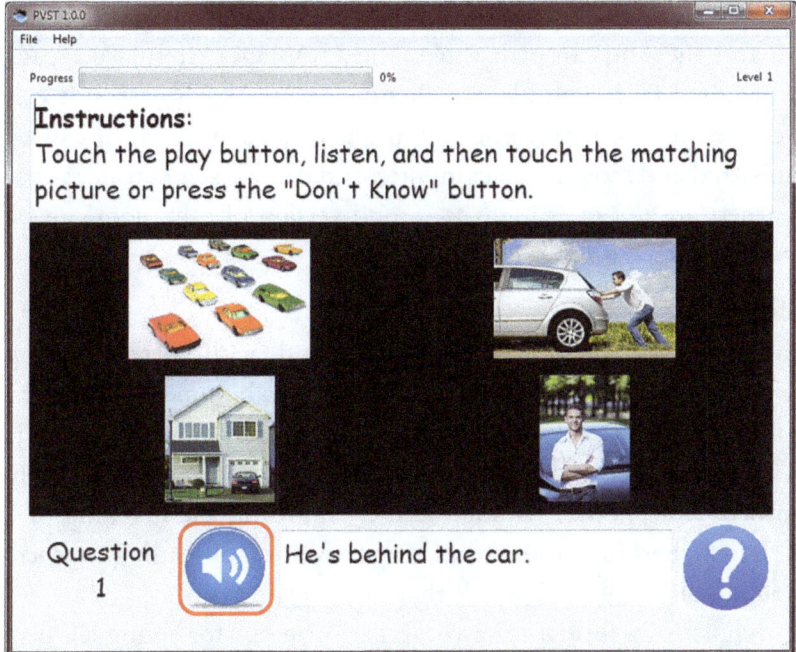

True/false tests

True/false tests involve the learner hearing a sentence and then deciding if it is true or false. It is also possible to include an 'I don't know' response. In the test, each word is tested twice in different sentences (see Box 4.1). This is to reduce the chances of guessing, because there is only a one-in-four chance of getting both answers correct.

Box 4.1 A true/false test

It is good to keep a <u>promise</u>.
People often <u>dream</u> when they are sleeping.
This is a <u>date</u>—10 o'clock.
When something is <u>impossible</u>, it is easy to do it.
<u>Milk</u> is blue.
When you <u>promise</u> something, you say you will really do it.
<u>Dreams</u> are about things that really happened.
When we give a <u>date</u>, we say the day, the month and the year.
It is <u>impossible</u> to live for a long time without water.
Very young children drink <u>milk</u>.

The disadvantages of this format are that the items are difficult to make (the contexts have to be easier words than the tested word); learners have to comprehend the sentence and relate it to their knowledge of the world, which means much more than vocabulary is being tested; and guessing can play a role. The advantages are that no reading is required (although like the Picture Vocabulary Size Test it can be presented in a written form), scoring is reliable and easy, it can be administered and scored on a computer, and if the tester considers that the learners are not guessing, the second version of each item can be omitted, thus saving time.

Reading aloud

Getting learners to read a list of words aloud, with correct reading being taken as evidence of knowing the word can be a measure of sight vocabulary (words that learners can sound out when reading), but it is not a measure of vocabulary size, because learners may be able to apply a knowledge of phonics without actually knowing the meaning of a word. Researchers have found that after a year or 2 of reading, learners can sound out many more words than they can explain.

The choice of a format for a vocabulary size test for young learners will depend on the goals of the testing. One major consideration will be if the tester wants to have a sensitive test or a tough test. A sensitive test provides a lot of support for the learner. It provides a sentence context (although this should be a non-defining context), it provides choices so that learners can draw on partial knowledge, and it keeps the learners motivated and on-task while doing the test. A tough test requires the learners to have a relatively strong knowledge of the word.

Assessing productive vocabulary

So far we have only considered receptive tests. Receptive tests require the learner to go from the word form to its meaning. This is the kind of knowledge needed for listening and reading. Oral receptive tests require listening knowledge of the spoken form of a word and its meaning. In contrast, productive tests require the learner to go from the meaning of a word to its form. This is the kind of knowledge needed for speaking and writing. It is probably not feasible to make productive vocabulary size tests for young learners who cannot read.

The Vocabulary Size Test (available from Paul Nation's website and online at http://www.my.vocabularysize.com) is a multiple-choice test going up to the 20,000 word level, but it requires learners to be able to read. This test has been used in research in New Zealand secondary schools and could also be used in upper primary school once learners are reading well.

Other than tests, there are three ways information about a learner's productive vocabulary knowledge can be gathered:

- by informally noticing a learner's use of vocabulary throughout a school day, talking with families about the learner's use of vocabulary at home, and (for other than the youngest of learners) asking the learner to make comments about their knowledge about words
- by assessing a learner's productive vocabulary as used in their spoken and written texts
- by assessing the vocabulary a learner knows before and after a topic has been covered.

Let's look at the last two of these.

Assessing a learner's productive vocabulary knowledge in text

A learner is asked to speak about a self-chosen and/or -nominated topic, or to speak in response to a photo prompt. Beforehand the learner is told what is being looked for: quality of expression, varied but relevant ideas, and using the 'best' word choices. The learner speaks a self-generated text (not in dialogue with the assessor) for as long as they are able, up to about 3–5 minutes' duration. The oral sample is recorded and transcribed. A second or third sample may be taken.

The transcribed text is put through the Vocabprofiler (kids)

(VP-Kids) program, an online analysis tool (http://www.lextutor.ca/vp/kids/), which breaks a text down into word frequencies based on 10 modified 250-word lists. Off-list known and unknown words are also identified. Available information includes a word count, a count of the different numbers of words used, and an analysis of how many words in each 250 band are in the text. This analytical approach is useful to gain insights into a learner's productive vocabulary use in text. Similarly, a learner's written text can be analysed by using VP-Kids to give insights into the vocabulary they use. An example follows. The student chose a photo of some children in an indoor swimming pool. The text of about 3.40 minutes, spoken by Andrew with the photo in front of him, was transcribed and put through the Vocabprofiler program.

Figure 4.2: Results from running a text through the Vocabprofiler program

Integral text: this picture is um a family that that was at the pool and there only one boy and five girls and so and all of them have has goggles so they can see underwater in the pool and the mum and dad are somewhere else in the picture and the boy is floating on the water and and two other girls and the the five other girls are floating on water too and a girl two girls have um really happy faces and the boy looks like he is closing his eyes and unknown the the water when he is floating the water looks really deep so they have those long things that can help them um float um on to surface of the water and their eyes are not open that much because the sun is blocking their eyes um making their eyes not see that much and they look like they are um about um like ten or fifteen or nine seven and it looks like they are the only their family is the only people at the pool and there and there only one girl wearing a necklace in the water

Analysis of the student's delivery of the text and the text itself suggests his text is not grammatically or lexically complex but this is not unusual when younger learners speak a continuous text about a topic. This student struggled to find explicit words for concepts he wished to convey, such as: the sun in their eyes; those long things. The text of 194 words has 80 different words, a small number of which are beyond the first 2,000 words in English: *goggles, underwater, blocking, necklace, surface*. When samples of a learner's spoken and written texts are analysed across time intervals in this way, using the Vocabprofiler, valuable information about the learner's productive vocabulary knowledge becomes available.

Assessing learners' vocabulary knowledge of a topic by collecting pre- and post-topic vocabulary knowledge

Insights into a learner's oral productive knowledge of words related to a topic or area of focus can be gathered by asking the learner to think of, then say, any words they know specifically related to a nominated topic. The person recording the learner's oral vocabulary should explain to the learner that the idea is to show off their knowledge of words about the topic—words that show their word knowledge about the topic.

It is helpful to model this using a different topic so that the learner gets the idea of what is required. For example: "For the topic *Cats*, the words I think of and can tell you are *fur, furry, chasing birds, hungry, purr, lick, sleeping, claws, scratching, pounce, my friend, kittens, tigers, different colours, long hair, short hair, tail, sharp ears*." You should explain that the words the learner says will be written down to record how clever the learner is with words about the topic. If the learner struggles, gently prompt them to keep thinking, to think of some more to say. If the learner continues to struggle and produces no new vocabulary, stop.

About 3 minutes is usually quite long enough to collect a good sample of the learner's word knowledge specific to a topic. It is highly likely that words they say are also understood. Noting the learner's degree of hesitancy and struggle, or confidence and fluency, alongside pronunciation effectiveness is helpful extra information. Collecting spoken samples of productive word knowledge before and after a topic in focus in the class offers evidence of uptake and learning.

A more generalised assessment sample of productive vocabulary knowledge can be taken by the learner nominating a topic, followed by one nominated by the person taking the sample. A learner's knowledge of productive vocabulary can also be gathered by the learner writing down the words they think of and know. The approach is much the same as above, except that the learner instead of the teacher writes the words down. The learner needs to know it is not a spelling test, and that if they struggle to spell the word they know, simply to give it their best spelling shot (see van Hees, 1999).

These oral or written productive vocabulary assessments merely give an indication of the learner's known and understood vocabulary in specific topic areas. Pre-topic samples indicate the learner's knowledge prior to a focus on the topic. Post-topic samples are particularly useful to gather insights into learning and uptake throughout a learning sequence.

A record of oral vocabulary (productive spoken knowledge) can be gathered across a wide spectrum of learners, including very young learners, new learners of English and writing-disabled learners. A record of written vocabulary (productive written knowledge) assumes the learner has enough knowledge about writing to at least attempt to write down readable words.

Implications for teaching and learning

1. An average 5-year-old native speaker of English who has grown up in a talking-focused and reading-focused family, has a vocabulary size of around 3,000 to 4,000 words and will increase this size by around 500–1,000 word families a year, at least until the end of their teenage years.

2. Some learners will have smaller vocabulary sizes, and because there is a very close relationship between vocabulary size and ease of reading, teachers should use a range of ways to help these learners reach a vocabulary size that is sufficient for reading appropriate for their age and stage. We will look at how to do this in the following chapters.

3. Teachers should use the Picture Vocabulary Size Test or the Vocabulary Size Test to measure the vocabulary size of some of their learners so they can get a feel for where their learners are in their vocabulary growth. It is best to do this testing individually for at least some of the learners.

4. Vocabulary knowledge can also be observed through getting learners to produce topic-related vocabulary before and after a topic is in focus in class. This can help assess the immediate effectiveness of content-based learning and the attention given to vocabulary throughout.

Further reading

For information about the vocabulary sizes of young native speakers in Canada, see:

A. Biemiller. (2005). Size and sequence in vocabulary development. In E. H. Hiebert & M. L. Kamil (Eds.), *Teaching and learning vocabulary: Bringing research into practice* (pp. 223–242). Mahwah, NJ: Lawrence Erlbaum Associates.

A. Biemiller, & N. Slonim. (2001). Estimating root word vocabulary growth in normative and advantaged populations: Evidence for a common sequence of vocabulary acquisition. *Journal of Educational Psychology, 93*(3), 498–520.

These researchers have carried out vocabulary size research in New Zealand secondary schools, which provides support for the rough rule of thumb for estimating vocabulary size:

A. Coxhead, P. Nation, & D. Sim. (2015). The vocabulary size of native speakers of English in New Zealand secondary schools. *New Zealand Journal of Educational Studies, 50*(1), 121–135.

J. van Hees. (1999). *Diagnostic oracy and literacy assessment in the four modes of listening, speaking, reading and writing.* Auckland: Auckland UniServices Ltd.

J. van Hees. (2011). *Oral expression of five and six year olds in low-socio economic schools.* Auckland: The University of Auckland. ResearchSpace@Auckland

For an example of a productive vocabulary size test, see:

B. Laufer, & P. Nation (1999). A vocabulary size test of controlled productive ability. *Language Testing, 16*(1), 36–55 (available free from Paul Nation's website http://www.victoria.ac.nz/lals/staff/paul-nation.aspx).

Resources

The Picture Vocabulary Size Test is available from Laurence Anthony's website (http://www.laurenceanthony.net/software/pvst/). For a true/false test of the first 1,000 words of English, see:

I. S. P. Nation. (1993). Measuring readiness for simplified material: A test of the first 1,000 words of English. In M. L.Tickoo (Ed.), *Simplification: Theory and application.* RELC Anthology Series no. 31 (pp. 193–203). Singapore: SEAMEO-RELC [available free from Paul Nation's website] http://www.victoria.ac.nz/lals/staff/paul-nation.aspx.

Chapter 5 Vocabulary and learning conditions

In Chapter 2 we looked at the need for learners to know most of the words (98% coverage) in the texts they read. In Chapter 4 we looked at learners' vocabulary sizes, and showed that most young native speakers have quite large vocabularies (several thousand words), which contain the majority of words they need to deal with in much of the reading they have to do when materials are appropriately selected. However, some learners will need support. In this chapter we look at the conditions affecting vocabulary learning. In the following chapters we look at how oral language, reading, and vocabulary teaching can help learners' vocabulary grow by setting up these conditions.

Conditions supporting vocabulary learning

Regardless of age, knowledge and learning context, there are general learning conditions that support vocabulary uptake and learning. These conditions are learner-oriented but not necessarily learner-determined. They may not occur if they have not been factored in by the teacher. These conditions include:

- being involved (participation and deliberate attention)
- having multiple encounters with the same words (repetition)
- paying attention to vocabulary (noticing)
- recalling knowledge from previous meetings (retrieval)
- enriching word knowledge through use in extended, meaningful contexts (varied meetings and varied use—repetition in new contexts)

- gaining new information about a word, such as its use in context, its word parts, its history, the patterns it fits into, and its core meaning (elaboration).

Teachers and well-designed texts can help these conditions occur, and learners can be shown how to encourage their occurrence.

- Effortful and purposeful interactional use encourages noticing and varied use.
- Facilitation through a mediating tool such as a person, task or activity can help meaningful noticing and retrieval.
- Large quantities of shared talk, audio listening and reading offer repeated encounters and varied use of the word.
- Extended talk involving the word offers elaborative meaning-making.
- Supportive, linked visuals enhance meaning and open up language possibilities.
- Shared reading with discussion of the text encourages deliberate attention and varied use.
- Dictionary use and explaining words helps deliberate attention and elaboration.
- Learning about word parts and word part analysis involves deliberate attention and elaboration.

In essence, vocabulary learning depends on multiple encounters with words and the quality of the meetings with each word.

Receptive and productive use

The receptive–productive distinction is related to each of the learning conditions (participation and deliberate attention, repetition, noticing, retrieval, varied receptive meetings and productive use in new contexts, and elaboration). Receptive knowledge involves being able to recognise the spoken or written form of the word when it is heard or seen and recall its meaning. Receptive knowledge is needed for listening and reading. Although young native speakers have little difficulty gaining receptive knowledge of the most useful words for listening, they need to develop sight vocabulary knowledge and reading fluency skills that will allow this receptive knowledge to be used when reading words in a text. Productive knowledge involves being able to recall the spoken or written word form in order to use it in context to express a meaning. Productive knowledge is needed for speaking and writing. Listening and reading are called the *receptive skills*, while speaking and writing are called the *productive skills*. Most times, spoken language is an integrated use of listening and speaking. However, at times, a person receives more than produces, for example, story telling. At other times, as in a balanced conversation, there is two-way speaking and listening.

Receptive knowledge is easier to gain than productive knowledge. Understanding a word in a receptive sense does not necessarily result in being able to use the word appropriately—productive knowledge. Productive knowledge requires greater and more detailed knowledge than receptive knowledge. For example, to understand a spoken word, we need to have some idea about what it sounds like and what it means. To produce a spoken word, we have to know which word best expresses the meaning we want and suits the context, and we need to have a clear idea of its pronunciation.

Table 5.1 summarises the conditions for vocabulary learning.

Table 5.1 The conditions for vocabulary learning

Learning condition	Receptive/productive	Explanation
Multiple encounters	Receptive	Meeting words a number of times when listening or reading
	Productive	Producing words a number of times when speaking and writing
Deliberate attention	Receptive attention Productive attention	Deliberately noticing or recalling the word's form, meaning or use
Noticing	Receptive	Paying attention to newly met words and being fascinated with words
	Productive	Noticing gaps in word knowledge
Retrieval	Receptive retrieval	Meaningfully engaging with words while listening or reading
	Productive retrieval	Using and trying out words in speaking or writing
Varied use	Varied receptive use Varied productive use	Meeting and producing words in varied spoken and written contexts
Elaboration	Receptive elaboration Productive elaboration	Learning more about the word, including its form, its meaning and its contextual use

The learning conditions in the table build on each other. Retrieval is a deeper condition than noticing. The condition of varied meetings and use involves retrieval, but is a deeper condition than retrieval because it involves variation. Elaboration can vary in depth but is typically the deepest. As Table 5.1 suggests, conditions involving receptive knowledge are not as deep as those involving productive knowledge.

Deliberate attention can occur across the levels of noticing, retrieval, varied meetings and use, and elaboration. Deliberate attention is more likely to result in learning than incidental learning, but both kinds of attention are valuable.

Applying the learning conditions

Multiple encounters (repetition) is a very important condition because it applies to all the other conditions. Repeated retrieval is much more effective in learning words than a single retrieval. Repeated deliberate noticing, especially spaced repeated attention, is much more effective than a single meeting. In this book the term *repetition* will largely be avoided in favour of expressions such as *multiple encounters*. This is because many teachers interpret *repetition* as doing exactly the same thing again: verbatim repetition. The most effective repetition, however, is meeting a word again in different forms, contexts, senses and texts. Looking at vocabulary learning in the most basic way, learning occurs because of multiple encounters and the quality of those encounters. Giving deliberate attention is one way of increasing quality. Retrieval, varied use and elaboration are other ways. Multiple encounters can be receptive (as in listening and reading) or productive (as in speaking and writing).

Deliberate attention sets up learners to be involved and so be focused on what is going on or being learned. It necessarily involves participation. For all learners, being involved in ways that are engaging and meaningful is likely to support their learning. The challenge for teachers is to involve all learners in participatory ways that hold their attention and sustain their focus. Learners who are minimally involved lose focus, their attention is lost, and the potential to learn available words slips away.

Deliberate attention includes word mindfulness by the teacher, and effortful noticing and involvement with the word by the learners. Teaching can involve working with learners to explain the meaning of a word; explaining words and giving an example; showing a visual (a drawing or photo or diagram) that clarifies the word in some way; or demonstrating the word's meaning through a gesture or action.

When learners ask the teacher or each other about words, when they look up the meaning of a word in a dictionary or discuss words together, when they research a word and report on their research, or when they try to memorise new words or play around with varied ways to use new words, there is deliberate attention to words by the learner.

Deliberate learning typically results in stronger learning than incidental learning, and is classified as part of the language-focused learning strand. However, it is important that there be a balance of vocabulary learning opportunities across the four strands of meaning-focused input, meaning-focused output, language-focused learning, and fluency development.

Most vocabulary learning by native speakers occurs not as a result of deliberate attention but through incidental learning. However, even in seemingly incidental learning, there are often degrees of deliberate attention and noticing. This is strongly seen when a very young child is learning the language. They are very alert to words and their meanings as used in their 'world' of living and being. Incidental learning occurs when meeting a word in reading, for example where the learner's focus is on the story not on vocabulary learning. The strands of meaning-focused input, meaning-focused output, and fluency development largely involve incidental learning.

Noticing occurs when learners give some attention to a word form and its meaning and use. Noticing is the starting point of all vocabulary learning because the deeper conditions of receptive and productive retrieval, and varied meetings and varied use, depend on previous noticing. Retrieval can only occur when something about the word has already been noticed and stored.

Most noticing is incidental and context-bound. That is, it occurs when the learner's attention is focused on something else besides a particular word, such as when the learner is focused on understanding instructions, or listening to a story, or being involved in a conversation, or reading. Noticing is strengthened if the teacher quickly notes a word up on the whiteboard or provides a quick explanation of the word, or illustrates it in some way to show the meaning of the word—through anecdote or example, or through a visual. Noticing is also encouraged when the teacher relates a newly met word to current knowledge.

Noticing is receptive when the learner gives attention to a word form and considers what it means. Noticing is productive when the learner wants to express a meaning but realises that the needed word is not known.

Noticing is an integral condition for learning. If noticing does not occur—especially for words that are on the edge of the learner's knowledge—the potential to learn the word may be lost. Deep learning is still several cumulative steps away through re-occurring meetings involving the other conditions of retrieval, varied meetings and use, elaboration and deliberate attention.

Receptive retrieval occurs when learners meet a word in spoken language or reading and have to recognise its form and recall its meaning, and use it in some way. This is why reading with and to children often gives them opportunities to use words supportively, and to remember and retrieve. It is very important that learners be given chances to recall and retrieve using their own effort, without someone stepping in too quickly to do the work for them. Providing assistance too quickly takes away the opportunity for the learner to put in the effort to retrieve and teaches them to feel comfortable with struggling.

If help is needed, it is preferable to supportively guide rather than simply provide the response. In this way, the learners draw on their own resources to make the retrieval rather than relying on others to do the work. A well-known reading support strategy is *pause, prompt and praise* (reinforce) in reading.

Sometimes covering up a visual in a print text is a useful way of forcing retrieval of the meaning. Emergent readers (especially) sometimes disproportionately rely on visual meaning to retrieve a word. By not seeing the visual, the learner needs to use the print text itself and so attends to the word in the text. Each successful retrieval results in a strengthening of the mental link between the word they know, the word form, and its meaning. Effort and connection by the learner to retrieve and make meaning is important.

Multiple read alouds and re-reading a text silently are effective ways of developing receptive retrieval fluency of words in print. Meaningfully engaging with oral texts is effective for developing spoken vocabulary retrieval.

Productive retrieval occurs when learners have a meaning to express and use a word in speaking or writing. Using or producing a word appropriately is more demanding than understanding vocabulary (receptive retrieval). Productive use of vocabulary requires independent control over word form and structure, meaning, and appropriate use in text and context. Recognising and understanding words and language requires interpreting effort only.

Many opportunities can be created where learners are supported to make successful productive retrievals. For example, orally, learners might share in pairs and in small or larger groups in turn-taking ways. Retelling a previously read story with the help of visuals from the story demands retrieval and reinforces word use and meaning-making. Retelling with language prompts and retelling after several readings is another retrieval strategy.

Varied receptive meetings help learning because they enrich the associations a particular word has and expand a learner's knowledge of use in meaningful contexts. When words recur in texts, they are typically in new or at least slightly different contexts from previous meetings with the same words. Meeting words from the same word family also provides varied meetings with the same base form. The major difference between receptive retrieval and varied receptive meetings is that varied receptive meetings involve retrieval in new contexts.

Reading in large quantities is a straightforward way of gaining lots of varied receptive meetings with words, and so it is a very useful way of expanding receptive vocabulary knowledge. This is especially so when the reading is on topics that are only partly familiar. Fortunately this is likely to be true for most factual and fiction reading that children do. Listening and discussion activities can also provide varied receptive meetings, but to help in vocabulary growth these spoken opportunities need to explore new ideas and push the learners beyond what they are very familiar with—working on the edge of their knowledge. Most of our daily speaking and listening involves what is very familiar. At school, learners should be challenged to go beyond this. There should be plenty of opportunities to learn vocabulary through engaging with spoken text in the Goldilocks zone of the learners.

Varied productive use involves taking risks with words by using them in ways they have not been met or used before by a particular learner. This is not as difficult as it sounds, because this is typical of most language use. The differences between the current use of a word's form and meaning and previous uses may be quite small; for example, changes between singular and plural, or between present and past tense, or first-person and third-person use. Similarly, what other words co-occur with a word may vary across texts; for example, a noun may occur with a different adjective or verb as in *a tennis ball, a golf ball hurtling towards me*; or a word can be used with a slightly different sense, such as *ball* referring to a tennis ball rather than a ball of fire.

When we talk or write about new topics, or when we talk or write about familiar topics from a different viewpoint, we are likely to make varied productive use of vocabulary. Linked skills activities, debates, re-enactments, role-playing, reporting, problem-solving discussions and a variety of conversational opportunities are all likely to encourage varied productive use of vocabulary.

Productive use has the advantage of strengthening both receptive and productive knowledge. Receptive use has the advantage of being very efficient: we can listen and read much more in the same time and with less effort than we can speak or write. However, it is not a competition between these two. Both are important in a well-balanced course.

Elaboration is a kind of varied use of words and has similar effects: it strengthens, enriches and expands vocabulary knowledge. It can focus on receptive knowledge or productive knowledge. Elaboration often requires some deliberate attention, and so it fits between incidental language use and deliberate attention. Here are some examples of providing elaboration.

1. The word is used in context. An expansion is made on the initial sentence or utterance to extend and build on the baseline idea and use offered. This is an important tool teachers should use with learners. By so doing, the sayer or contextual use is foregrounded and enhanced, offering additional knowledge to the learner.
2. The learner sees a visual that illustrates part of the text containing a new or partly known word or the word itself.
3. The learner imagines an image illustrating a word.
4. The teacher and the learners work together to create a semantic map

on the whiteboard, which links the important ideas and vocabulary related to a topic. A semantic map involves listing important ideas and arranging them and drawing lines between them to show their relationship. Semantic mapping is described in Chapter 8 and in Appendix 6.

5. The learners classify several uses of a word into two or three different groups according to a given criterion; for example, whether the uses apply to living things or non-living things, or according to the grammar of the word. For example, the use of the word *cup* in *She cupped her hands* refers to a living thing.
6. The teacher breaks a word into word parts and explains how the parts relate to the meaning of the word.
7. The teacher gives some other sense-making uses of the word and shows how they all share a common meaning. For example, *an arch* can be part of a building, but a cat can also *arch* its back. These two senses refer to the same shape.

Elaboration activities enrich vocabulary knowledge. They can enrich knowledge of the form, meaning and use of a word.

We have looked at a range of vocabulary-learning conditions—from noticing to retrieval, from varied use to elaboration and deliberate attention. The reason for looking at them is that vocabulary learning occurs not because of any particular hidden magic but because these conditions are at work. It is important to understand these conditions so that learning and teaching activities can be analysed and observed to see if the conditions are occurring. If they are not occurring, then some adjustments will need to be made to the activities or approach to make sure that favourable conditions for learning occur. Understanding the conditions needed for learning allows teachers and learners to manage what they do so that learning is most likely to occur.

Further reading

For a more detailed discussion of the conditions affecting vocabulary learning, see Chapter 1 of:

I. S. P. Nation, & S. Webb. (2011). *Researching and analyzing vocabulary.* Boston, MA: Heinle Cengage Learning.

The chapter includes an elaborate checklist of conditions for analysing vocabulary learning activities. This kind of analysis is called *technique feature analysis.*

The following book contains a detailed analysis of a wide range of techniques for learning vocabulary, looking at the conditions involved and how they can be encouraged:

S. Webb, & I. S. P. Nation. (2017). *How vocabulary is learned.* Oxford, UK: Oxford University Press.

Chapter 6 Oral language and vocabulary growth

Communication using words that are spoken in some way involves using oral language. It assumes speaking and listening are involved in some form, even when talking to oneself, as in child self-talk. People primarily use oral language when talking with others face-to-face or through some other dynamic tools such as Skype or the telephone. For learners, frequent quality conversations with another person scaffolding their talk are critically important to develop their vocabulary knowledge.

Oral language is widely used and available in a variety of forms and contexts, and there are many opportunities for learners to engage with oral language through technology. Ideally, learners should have plenty of opportunities to be involved in oral language through talk with a wide variety of people in meaningful contexts, by listening to others in face-to-face contexts, and through technology. All are important, and together they offer potentially rich vocabulary learning opportunities. Interestingly, however, recent neuroscience research shows clearly that for young children, at least, a person (or face-to-face interactant) is a necessary requirement for language attention and uptake.

Talking and vocabulary learning

A very young child's vocabulary knowledge and use have been derived almost solely from oral sources, especially through talking with others. Through frequent and varied conversations with others, with the child contributing in a weave of meaningful talk with another person, the child gradually builds up a word bank of around 3,000 words by the age of 5. For maximum gain in vocabulary and language growth, it is important that these talking exchanges are varied and extending in some way, with the child having the chance to learn new words from them.

Oral language is the major source of vocabulary growth for young children before they go to school, and it continues to play an important role throughout their lives, even when they have learned to read. An environment of oral language that develops a child's vocabulary might be like this:

- A person is responsively engaged with the child, scaffolding their talk.
- There are frequent replies to the child's talk.
- The child is given space and frequent opportunities to speak.
- Speech is frequently addressed to the child.
- Longer utterances (extended speech) are appropriately used with the child, offering the child language that is slightly more complex than their own capability.

There are conversational features with a learner that are associated with potentially rich vocabulary learning. Scaffolding is important because it 'gifts' the child new words and expressions that are likely to be noticed and understood. Gifting more words in well-structured expression-extending speech inevitably gifts more word knowledge and more concepts. When the exchange of meaning is in the learner's Goldilocks zone—not too simple, not too complex; not too long, not too short; not too quickly, not too slowly—and in an environment where the learner engages with the language because the context is relevant and connected to the child, acquiring the words used by another is more likely to occur. The 'new' can become the learner's known.

Ideally, many oral exchanges with learners—at any age—are elaborative in some way. The regular availability of elaborative expression from another, with the learner actively involved in the talk, can significantly contribute to increasing their vocabulary resources. Alongside receiving language, the learner also needs many opportunities to participate by speaking. The learner expressing is important so that they can try out and consolidate the newly available vocabulary.

In the classroom, elaborative conversational exchanges are more than possible; they are necessary for learners to gain vocabulary through talk in the context of teaching and learning. While a class group has many individuals, engaging in elaborative exchanges of talk in class can become the norm. In classrooms where teaching and learning are largely conversational or dialogic, and where all the learners receive and try elaborated, extending ways of talking, vocabulary learning opportunities abound (see van Hees, 2007).

Gifting conversational exchanges

By way of illustrating the less and more of talk with a learner, consider two conversational exchanges between a mother and child, with more or less elaboration from the mother. Here is a simple talk exchange:

Child: Mum, I'm hungry.

Mother: Here's a banana then.

Child: I don't want a banana. Look in here.

(The child goes to the pantry to find something else.)

Mother: No, eat this or nothing.

Child: I don't like a banana. A bikkie.

Mother: No bikkie. The banana or forget about it.

Child: You're mean, mummy.

(38 words in total)

Here is a more elaborative, extending and responsive talk exchange:

Child: Mum, I'm hungry.

Mother: There's a lovely ripe banana in the bowl right there for you to eat. Lucky you.

Child: I don't want a banana. Look in here.

(The child goes to the pantry to find something else.)

Mother: It's a banana for you right now or you'll have to wait till lunchtime for a sandwich. Look how deliciously ripe the banana is ... just waiting for a little monkey like you to eat it.

Child: I'm not a monkey. I don't want a banana.

Mother: So, no banana. Maybe if we go to the zoo on Sunday we could give it to a hungry monkey. You'll have to wait till lunchtime for a sandwich. Then you can choose what you would like on your sandwich.

Child: Can I? Yum. I want cheese and Marmite.

(126 words in total)

In the simple exchange the child receives a very limited number of words from the mother, limiting the quantity of speech heard and the number of concepts available to them. Eighty-three percent of the words are within the first 250-word range in English, with *banana* and *hungry* within the 750–1,000-word range, and '*bikkie*' (or biscuit) at the 2,000+ high-frequency word level.

The child interacting with her mother in the elaborative exchange would have heard or used triple the number of words compared with the child in the simple exchange. The concepts are richer and more complex, as is the language structure, particularly as used by the mother. In contrast to the simple exchange, in the elaborative exchange, there are 18 words above the first 250 words in English—*lovely, monkey, till, wait, bowl, maybe, Sunday, banana, cheese, Marmite, hungry, sandwich, lucky, choose, ripe, lunchtime, deliciously* and *yum*.

Imagine 20 such exchanges between mother and child in a day. The child in elaborated exchanges would hear and use 360 words above the first 250 words in English, compared to 40 such words in the simple exchanges. Over a year the child in the elaborative exchanges would have heard or used significantly more complex vocabulary than the child in the simple exchanges. Over time this would result in marked differences between the vocabulary knowledge of one child compared to the other.

Other oral language sources

Songs, storytelling (face-to-face, or radio, or on digital devices), rhymes and chants, hymns and prayers, broadcasted news for children, YouTube clips, computer games and interactive materials are examples of commonly available oral texts in most countries of the world.

When available in ways that engage the learner in meaningful comprehension, all these sources have the potential to expand a learner's vocabulary knowledge.

Listening to learner-engaging, audio-only texts, for example on radio, offers learners potentially rich sources of vocabulary. Analysing a radio broadcast text for children (for example, *Cocky*) illustrates this vividly.

> I knew it was going to be a bad day when the lady took one look at me and screamed. So I'm a cockroach, I thought. Big deal. You know, the city can be a lonely place. The lady and I had been sharing the same kitchen for months and yet I was a stranger to her. I felt sorry for the lady—I mean, she only had two legs. Look, I said, I know a great place for leftover pizza. How about we take a few minutes out of our busy lives and get to know each other? The lady ran out of the room. Strange, I thought. Maybe she doesn't like pizza? You know I might be just an ordinary little guy but I've got friends in high places. See that spider on the ceiling? That's Daddy. Ah, he's not my father, of course, but his name's Daddy Long Legs so we call him Daddy for short. Living way up there he gets a great view of the kitchen and often drops by to tell me about bits of food I might have missed. A smear of vegemite on the door handle, dried up noodles from down the side of the stove, and for my part, I try to send the odd fly his way. Never tried them myself, but hey—I'm always willing to broaden my horizons.
>
> *1.48 mins,*
>
> *230 words*
>
> Source: R. Nathan, *Storytime treasure chest*. Radio NZ National. Retrieved 10 October 2014, from http://podcast.radionz.co.nz/misc/misc-20081105-0900-Cocky-048.mp3

Analysed using VP-KIDS profiler, the majority of words are from the first 500 words in English. However, there are also 25 words above the first 1,000 words in English. Can you identify them?

With just under 2 minutes of listening, a learner engaged with this story through listening is exposed to more higher-level vocabulary than they are likely hear in a 2-minute day-to-day conversational exchange. *Cocky* is a written text, even though the main character tells the story in a conversational way. Its literacy-related features include expanded concepts, writing-like syntax, more words than would be likely to be said in 2 minutes of conversation, and a significant number of higher-level words.

Imagine a learner listening with meaning to 10 minutes of audio-only texts every day, five times a week, 40 weeks a year. Assuming such texts might offer at least as many vocabulary items above the first 1,000 words in English as the *Cocky* text, there could potentially be 100 words above the first 1,000 over 5 days, and 4,000 such words across 40 weeks of a year available for learning. Such vocabulary availability will have a considerable impact on a learner's potential vocabulary knowledge.

Figure 6.1 A vocabulary levels analysis of a text using Vocabprofiler

1st 250	2nd 250	3rd 250	4th 250	5th 250	6th 250	7th 250	8th 250	9th 250	Off list
TYPES 89	16	7	6	4	4	1	2	3	10

Page Menu: Tokens Types Families

Integral text: i knew it was going to be a bad day when the lady took one look at me and screamed so i am a cockroach i thought big deal you know the city can be a lonely place the lady and i had been sharing the same kitchen for months and yet i was a stranger to her i felt sorry for the lady i mean she only had two legs look i said i know a great place for leftover pizza how about we take a few minutes out of our busy lives and get to know each other the lady ran out of the room strange i thought maybe she does not like pizza you know i might be just an ordinary little guy but i have got friends in high places see that spider on the ceiling that is daddy ah he is not my father of course but his name daddy long legs so we call him daddy for short living way up there he gets a great view of the kitchen and often drops by to tell me about bits of food i might have missed a smear of vegemite on the door handle dried up noodles from down the side of the stove and for my part i try to send the odd fly his way never tried them myself but hey i am always willing to broaden my horizons

Storytime Treasure Chest, produced by Radio New Zealand,[1] is an example of a high-quality, non-commercial, audio-only resource available to young learners through radio-live listening or delayed listening as podcasts. Other public broadcasting services around the world also cater for children as listeners. The BBC, for example, has a number of audio and movie productions for young listeners.[2] Regular listening to such well-produced audio-texts for children is extremely useful. These broadcasts and podcasts offer children elaborative oral language, grammatically more complex language structures, conceptual richness, and potentially extending vocabulary.

Young learners and newer learners of English benefit when what they are listening to is talked about along the way and afterwards. This allows for clarifying what they don't understand, gives them an opportunity to process what they are hearing, and allows for words and ideas

---

1 http://www.radionz.co.nz/collections/storytime-treasure-chest
2 http://www.bbc.co.uk/podcasts/genre/childrens

to be foregrounded. Too much pausing will make for disjointed listening, however, so prudent use of chatting moments during the audio is recommended.

It is easiest to pause and chat along the way when the audio is not in real time, as in podcasts. Teachers using *Storytime Treasure Chest* audios with small groups of learners, as well as with large class groups, are having great success with this approach. What has become evident is that many learners have significant gaps in their conceptual and informational knowledge, struggle with expressions and the ways language is used, and often lack vocabulary knowledge. Done well, this talk before, during and after listening to audios excites the learners. They love these meaningful interactions with a story with some talking along the way, and are making gains in vocabulary, language expression and concepts knowledge.

The important point is that a learner who engages in meaningful ways with non-conversational, literacy-like oral texts stands to gain knowledge of many words over and above words available in day-to-day conversations. However, simply being immersed in an oral language text is no guarantee that the words a learner is exposed to because they are there will be learned. Without meaningfully engaging with the text and noticing words, the potential to learn these words is lowered. Somehow the learner needs to be cognitively engaged with the oral text and comprehending to a great extent.

Multimedia oral language sources

Digital devices and the internet have made available to young learners a wide variety of multimedia texts in which oral language features or plays an integral part. There are rich pickings. Well-produced movie clips for children appeal, and are potentially a powerful means to develop their vocabulary knowledge. While many such clips and resources may be commercial, there are literally thousands of quality clips suitable for children freely available on YouTube. Outside schooling, learners may have more or less ready access to such movie clips. In the classroom, everyone can have access.

Not all movie clips for children on the internet are of equal quality or appropriateness. What to select depends on the learners and what is relevant to the learning in hand. Careful selection of the 'just right' movies for your learners is time well spent. Criteria to keep in mind include:

- length—a lengthier clip may need to be viewed in bite-size portions
- an audio script that is in the Goldilocks zone of the learners—not too complex to be above their capability, and not too simple, so that it provides them with potential new vocabulary learning
- in-built redundancy, so the learners have plenty of opportunity to connect the visual images and the audio, and encounter vocabulary and concepts several times over
- topics that are appealing and relevant to the learners.

Explicit attention to the vocabulary in a movie clip

Here are some suggested steps for enhancing the vocabulary learning potential of movies.

1. Build background knowledge with your learners prior to movie viewing and listening. This will bring to the fore ideas and vocabulary relevant to the movie contents and topic.
2. Focus on the meaning-carrying words in the title to connect to the movie contents.
3. Depending on the length and complexity of the movie, either:

    (a) get learners to watch the movie through without the teacher pausing the clip, to get the gist of the movie and try to extract information and understanding on the first view and listen, and follow this by a discussion of what the learners have been able to extract, as well as identifying queries and gaps; and follow this with view and process segment-by-segment as below, or

    (b) get learners to watch the movie in segments, focusing on the ideas and vocabulary of each segment, followed later by a complete viewing and discussion—this approach means that deeper meaning can be gained all along the way, culminating in more meaningful whole-movie viewing.

PowerPoint is a useful tool to use to scaffold learners through the movie as in 1 and 2 above. The movie hyperlink is embedded into the PowerPoint at timely places. Alongside shorter or longer movie-clip viewing, the transcribed audio script can also be presented. The capturing of the spoken text as print offers learners a reading opportunity and greater uptake potential because the text is slowed down. Key vocabulary in the script can be in freeze-frame focus, with key word or word groups highlighted for noticing and attention.

Here is an example. The learning focus in this class of 7- to 8-year-olds is 'How a plant grows from a seed'. Obviously, a focus on the 'real' is part of their learning journey. As part of the scaffolding, and to increase the meaningful learning of topic-specific vocabulary and language, the *How does a seed grow?* YouTube video was used.[3] The movie depicts core knowledge about how a plant grows from a seed, using fast-moving, simple, kid-friendly whiteboard animation, accompanied by a spoken text. It should be noted that only low levels of noticing and learning of new and expanding vocabulary available in the commentary are likely if the spoken text of the movie is not slowed down, foregrounded and unpacked with the learners. When this is done, however, learners are likely to learn new vocabulary and reinforce partially known vocabulary that would otherwise flash by them, or only be partially grasped. An example follows.

In the first 44 seconds of the 2-minute movie, core knowledge about a seed is introduced. The animation is accompanied by the following spoken text:

> Plants are all around us. Almost all these plants come from seeds. Ever wonder how a plant grows from just a single seed? Seeds come in all shapes and sizes—from very small to very large. Let's take a closer look at this bean seed. Seeds have a protective outer layer called the seed coat. The seed coat protects the seed from predators, bad weather or drying out. If we look inside the seed, we can see that most of the seed is made up of the seed's food, called endosperm. The endosperm is coloured yellow. Endosperm is mostly made up of oils, sugars or proteins. In the middle of all this endosperm is the baby plant.

The learners and teacher talk about what they already know about how seeds grow, watch the movie all the way through, share understanding extracted from viewing it once, and watch the movie segment-by-segment, accompanied by discussion and an explicit focus on spoken text vocabulary. The spoken vocabulary becomes more noticeable because segment-by-segment, the spoken text is transcribed for learners to notice in print form. Vocabulary of note can be bolded for extra attention and noticing.

---

3   https://www.youtube.com/watch?v=lGCZXx_Pczo

After one shared reading of the text, the text is shown again, this time with some key vocabulary bolded for noticing and attention, as below:

> Plants are all around us. Almost all these plants come from seeds. **Ever wonder** how a plant grows from **just a single seed**? Seeds come in all **shapes and sizes**—from very small to very large. Let's take **a closer look** at this bean seed. Seeds have **a protective outer layer** called **the seed coat**. The seed coat **protects** the seed from **predators, bad weather** or **drying out**. If we look inside the seed, we can see that most of the seed is made up of the seed's food, called endosperm. The endosperm is coloured yellow. Endosperm is mostly made up of oils, sugars or proteins. In the middle of all this endosperm is the baby plant.

A suggested approach is for learners in pairs to identify one of the bolded words or word groups, read the contextual sentence, and together either prepare an explanation or meaning comment, or simply say something about the concepts. These are then shared as a class, turn-taking pairs identifying, commenting and explaining theirs, with the other learners also contributing. Those not identified by learner pairs are considered together as a class.

Done well, this slowing down and explicit attention to the vocabulary in the spoken movie text enhances learner understanding and remembering of the text's parts and whole. It supports uptake and learning of potentially available vocabulary that might otherwise go unnoticed or be minimally understood.

Learners engaging with multimedia texts where images, print and spoken texts merge can be a great source of vocabulary learning. However, hearing the text and exposure is not enough for learning to occur and may well not result in learners learning vocabulary. This is especially true of spoken texts accompanied by moving images. Much language and potentially available vocabulary will simply pass learners by without guided attention to text parts other than the images.

Further reading

M.A.K. Halliday. (1985). *Spoken and written language.* Waum Ponds, VIC: Deakin University.

E. Hoff. (2006). How social contexts support and shape language development. *Developmental Review, 26*(1), 55–88.

Chapter 7 Vocabulary and reading

In this chapter we discuss reading as a major source of vocabulary learning. In particular, we consider guided or shared reading, and apply vocabulary learning conditions to an analysis of a reading activity. We also look at how much reading learners need to do. One of the goals of this chapter is to show that frameworks that we have looked at earlier in this book, namely the conditions for learning and the four strands, relate to language learning through reading and more generally across the four skills of listening, speaking, reading and writing.

Reading mileage

An appetite for reading is seeded in a child's early years. Children who are read to and read from an early age (it's never too young to start) are likely to learn many words they might otherwise not learn through conversational talk. Engaging with audio-books and reading to and with a young child in an engaging way usually involves 'to and fro' talking—conversation. Conversations may occur when looking at the book's visuals, when reading the text itself, and when discussing words arising through the visuals and text. Often these text-specific words are ones that are not used in everyday talk exchanges between adults and children. Through books, and literacy-like audio texts, children have opportunities to meaningfully hear, see and to learn words less frequently used in everyday speech.

Ideally, all children should continue to be avid readers as they grow through their later childhood years and into adulthood. Extensive and intensive recreational reading will inevitably result in the child gaining vocabulary knowledge—knowledge about a word's form, its meanings and its use in text. Low reading mileage and restricted reading of text types and topics usually mean restricted higher-level vocabulary learning opportunities. Stimulating and supporting learners to read recreationally—ideally daily for at least 30 minutes per day—and to choose books across a range of factual and fiction texts is an important way to support vocabulary learning.

Alongside a rich diet of reading, children who engage with quality spoken texts with more complex language structure and higher-level vocabulary—literacy-like texts that are delivered in oral form—are likely to learn many words that are advanced yet learnable because they are meaningful and relevant to the child in context.

Guided or shared reading

Guided or shared reading is an integral part of a reading instruction programme in most primary school classrooms. It is a kind of intensive reading where the teacher elaborates on a text with the learners, focusing on learners understanding the text more deeply and fully. Usually shared reading involves rich discussion and sharing of ideas in the text and beyond. Often attention is drawn to language features such as vocabulary, interesting expressions, and grammatical structures in the text. Shared reading provides a chance to meet new and partly known words in a supportive context. If the teacher discusses the text with the learners, this provides an opportunity for varied use of the words.

There is no single instructional reading method, but certain features and steps are common across particular ways of reading instructionally with learners. The following are the main features of shared reading.

Instructional level

For a text to be instructional, the text content and written text need to be at the far edge of the current level of the learners' knowledge. That is, without some support and guidance, the learners would not be able to fully grasp the contents nor manage the print text fluently and with comprehension.

Scaffolding for fluency and meaning-making

There is a recommended sequenced order to work with learners during guided or shared reading.

1. Talk about the title and what this suggests the book might be about.
2. Pay attention to the contents page and index (if available) and discuss what is likely to be in the book.
3. Talk about the learner's current concepts and knowledge of the overall topic of the text.
4. Along the way, weave in opportunities for learners to share their specific thinking and knowledge, perceptions and understanding, stimulated directly or indirectly by the visuals or text.
5. Focus specifically on the diagrams or photos or pictures, talk about them, exploring what is there, but also any matters or thoughts related to them but not directly there.
6. If the book is a factual text, you might select a specific part of the book to focus on, or begin by getting the idea of the book as a whole, then read sections in more depth. If it is a fiction or story text, start at the beginning.
7. Along the way, identify and discuss any key vocabulary that is difficult, or important, or interesting.
8. Use the text and shared understanding about words to explore important or new or difficult words, and at times consult a dictionary.
9. One option is for the learners to read parts together, or initially read a part silently before shared reading. They may take turns to read aloud around the group, with or without support. This is an opportunity to develop learners' reading fluency, alongside reading for meaning.
10. Reading for meaning is the ultimate goal of reading, and so discussing meaning and text features that convey these along the way is most important.
11. Talk about what is important and why, and what is interesting and why. Discuss reactions and thoughts together. Open up opportunities for learners to share what they know, what they are thinking, and what they notice in the text.
12. Rich discussion throughout shared reading offers opportunities to consider vocabulary in the text and use related words in talk.

Ideally, the teacher is ready to 'gift' learners new words and ways of expressing, and to support learners to share and notice their collective vocabulary knowledge.

Big book shared reading

In junior-level classes, typically the teacher might select what is often called a 'big book': a very large-sized version of a children's book. The book is usually clearly in view of the learners so they can see the words and the pictures. The book-reading session in many ways resembles what might occur in the home when parents or family members read with a child. The adult and child interact with the contents of the book through conversation and talk. The steps above are basically followed, but with young children especially there is much spontaneity and responsiveness by and with the children.

Shared reading is appropriate and useful for older learners, and can be just as effective as with young children. The recommended steps described above also work for older learners reading more sophisticated and complex texts. The teacher ought to work with learners in a lively and conversational manner, not prescriptively, but keeping in mind the basic principles and steps of shared reading: to build reading-for-meaning and the vocabulary knowledge and thinking of the learners. Reading with older learners needs to be a positive experience, which is involving and participatory.

Vocabulary learning through shared reading

Research on shared reading shows that it results in vocabulary learning, especially for receptive knowledge, and if the learners are given a chance to produce the words during the shared reading session through conversational talk it can contribute to productive knowledge as well. By engaging in rich discussion throughout, with all learners involved, optimal conditions for learning are triggered.

Shared reading provides a chance to meet new and partly known words in a supportive context. If the teacher discusses the text with the learners, this provides an opportunity for varied use of the words. For young learners especially, who often like hearing the same story several times, reading the same story again can provide excellent opportunities for repeated retrieval of previously met vocabulary. If the teacher encourages the learners to use the words in the story when talking about it, this provides the very deep condition of varied productive use.

Elaboration and extension can occur if the teacher relates the words to the book visuals, or to the learners' current knowledge and experience. The teacher can help the learners give deliberate attention to words in the book by discussing or giving their meaning, perhaps noting them up on the board to enhance noticing, and talking with learners about them. The main purpose of shared reading is to get learners excited about reading, but with a little bit of careful thought it can be used to significantly contribute to vocabulary learning.

The findings of research on shared reading agree with the analysis of the vocabulary learning conditions described in Chapter 5 in that deliberate attention, noticing, varied use and elaboration all improve learning from shared reading.[1]

A well-balanced reading programme

Digital texts are increasingly available and used in classrooms and by learners, so it is important to consider any discussion about reading as being generally applicable to both a more traditional medium such as print on paper and digitally available texts. The medium is different, but approaches used with either are transferable.

In a well-balanced reading programme there should be three kinds of reading: (1) reading where the learner is reading for meaning and doing this independently, (2) reading such as shared reading and intensive reading, where reading occurs with plenty of external support, and (3) fluent reading, where the learner reads very easy material in order to increase reading fluency.

Table 7.1 compares these three kinds of reading.

---

[1] For example Pollard-Durodola, S. D., Gonzalez, J. E., Simmons, D. C., Kwok, O., Taylor, A. B., Davis, M. J., ... & Simmons, L. (2011). The effects of an intensive shared book-reading intervention for preschool children at risk for vocabulary delay. *Exceptional Children*, *77*(2), 161-183.
Evans, M. A., Williamson, K., & Pursoo, T. (2008). Preschoolers' attention to print during shared book reading. *Scientific Studies of Reading*, *12*(1), 106-129.

Table 7.1 The three kinds of reading in a well-balanced reading course

Type of reading	Nature of reading	Reading speed	Reading activities
Independent reading	Reading material that contains only a few unfamiliar features	150–250 words per minute (wpm)	Reading for pleasure Reading for study Narrow reading
Intensive reading	Reading challenging material with attention to features of the text that contribute to meaning, usually interacting with the teacher or class mates. This may be done independently with support from a dictionary, for example	100 wpm or less	Intensive reading Shared reading Pair reading Reciprocal reading
Reading for fluency	Reading very easy, familiar material, usually with some pressure to go faster	250–300 wpm	Reading easy books Re-reading the same books Repeated reading Speed reading

Reading for pleasure may or may not be fully independent. Younger children will most usually enjoy reading for pleasure when in the company of someone who reads the book with them. As children grow more independent as readers, their reading for pleasure choices and extent will hopefully grow and vary.

Reading for study in primary schools usually refers to cross-curricula reading—the reading that occurs throughout teaching and learning tasks and focuses. Narrow reading involves reading within a very restricted topic area. This is so that the reading becomes easier because the learners very quickly become familiar with the topic and there is a chance of encountering topic-related vocabulary a number of times. Pair reading involves two learners sitting together reading the same text and helping each other when necessary. The reading may be done aloud or silently. Reciprocal reading is where learners work in pairs or small groups to follow a set procedure for understanding a text. A basic guide is: http://www.educationscotland.gov.uk/Images/ReciprocalReadingGuide_tcm4-812956.pdf

As a part of reading for fluency, re-reading the same books and repeated reading are not the same. Re-reading involves reading books that were read some time in the past, a few weeks or months ago.

Repeated reading involves reading the same text three times one after the other in the same reading session. There are specially designed speed reading courses, sometimes called timed reading, for native speakers and speed reading courses in a controlled vocabulary for learners of English as a foreign language (see Paul Nation's website). They all involve passages of a set length accompanied by multiple-choice questions. When learners read their speed is timed, converted to words per minute, and entered on a personal graph.

We can analyse vocabulary learning from independent reading and reading for fluency in the same way as we looked at shared reading. Table 7.2 includes this analysis.

Table 7.2 Conditions for vocabulary learning in the three kinds of reading

Type of reading	Features of the type of reading	Conditions for vocabulary learning
Independent reading	Silent reading Dictionary use or referral to a person	Receptive retrieval Receptive varied use Deliberate attention
Intensive reading	Explaining words together Discussion of the text Re-reading the same text	Deliberate attention Receptive and productive varied use Receptive retrieval
Reading for fluency	Reading several times over Large quantities of easy reading	Receptive retrieval Receptive varied retrieval

Note that all of the above conditions should provide opportunities to re-encounter words. Meeting new or partially known words a number of times in text supports learning.

Notice, too, that in independent reading, if the learner does not look up words or ask someone to explain them, the learning conditions are receptive retrieval and receptive varied use. These learning conditions are not among the strongest learning conditions, and so independent reading typically results in small amounts of vocabulary learning. If, however, learners read in large quantities, somewhere around an hour a day, then large amounts of vocabulary learning can occur. This is because words occurring in different texts then becomes a significant factor in vocabulary learning because the quantity of reading allows words to be met many times. Vocabulary learning from input is a cumulative process, with each meeting of a partly known word likely to add to knowledge of the word.

Fluency development in reading requires easy material, some push to read faster than usual, a strong focus on the message of the text, and large quantities of such reading. Because the material is easy and familiar, there is little need for deliberate attention so most learning is incidental involving receptive retrieval and receptive varied retrieval.

Let's now look at how books written for children set up good conditions for reading and for vocabulary learning.

How children's books support vocabulary learning

Look at the complete texts of three early-reading children's books: *Flowers*, *Playing*, and *Watching TV*. Which one most supports vocabulary learning?

Table 7.3 The complete texts of three early reading books

Flowers	Playing	Watching TV
This is a red flower.	I like to run.	The moon.
This is a yellow flower.	I like to hide.	The astronaut.
This is a white flower.	I like to slide.	The space monster.
This is a blue flower.	I like to jump.	The superwoman.
This is a purple flower.	I like to swing.	The spaceships.
This is a pink flower.	I like to crawl.	"Go to bed!" said Mom.
This is a bunch of flowers.	I like my bath best of all!	"Ohhhh! Mom!"

Source: The stories are from the Reading Oceans series from Compass Publishing.

Each of the three texts has a visual alongside each sentence. This assists the learner to work out the words using the visual as a clue. However, the learner may be relying on the visual to make good or correct guesses for words they would otherwise not recognise or be able to read. In that sense, they may know the word because they understand and identify it through the visuals, but not have read-only control over and comprehension of the word.

It is important to realise that guessing and remembering the words based on the visual is not reading words. For young learners, the teacher needs to be vigilant in order to notice learners appearing to read the words when in fact they are simply using the visual cue and remembering. To support learners to read the actual words, spaced re-readings and covering the visuals are useful strategies.

The text *Watching TV* may have too heavy a vocabulary load for very young learners, with each line of text containing what may be a new word with a complicated meaning. However, if learners are interested in the topic, they may well handle these words both for meaning and reading fluency in text. Both *Flowers* and *Playing* may have one or two new words or partly known words (*purple, slide, crawl*) and meeting them in the stories can enrich the learners' vocabulary. For some young learners who do not know the colours well, *Flowers* may consolidate their knowledge of the word *flower*, and potentially they can learn some or all the colour words in the story. If only one (or at most two) of the colours are not well known, then *Flowers* is probably the best text for vocabulary learning because of the large amounts of repetition. *Playing* is a very close second.

It is important to provide varied and enticing reading for young learners. The above three texts may seem 'rather boring' to a capable young thinker and early reader. Part of the course of learning to read, however, is to start with simple text with familiar vocabulary and ideas that support the early reader to build their reading knowledge of words. Care should be taken that this does not become tedious for the young learner. They will thrive on being involved in reading books that tell more and excite and interest them alongside 'learning to read' texts.

How could a book like *Playing* be used to maximise vocabulary learning while still keeping the children's interest? The way to maximise vocabulary learning is to make sure the conditions of retrieval, varied use, elaboration and deliberate attention occur, and that there are opportunities to meet the target words a number of times under these conditions. When the print text is monotonous and predictable, but provides a supportive text for an emergent reader, the accompanying talk about the meaning-carrying words and visuals are major ways to hold the learner's interest and offer vocabulary-extending opportunities beyond the text.

An obvious way to build multiple encounters with words is to come back to the same book or text several times. One approach is to introduce the book or text in shared reading, use it in shared reading two or three times, make the text available for independent reading, and then some time later encourage learners to re-read it quickly for fluency development. This need not be done with every book or text, but it is a useful sequence because it provides opportunities for repetition, although it involves retrieval without varied meetings.

Another helpful approach is to make the book or text the focus of a linked set of tasks. This involves dealing with the same topic (the content of the book or text) across three of the four skills of listening, speaking, reading and writing, so that re-encountering words receptively and productively becomes part of the activity. The learners could listen to the teacher read the book or text accompanied by lots of talk, read the text for themselves, write in some way related to the text, possibly followed by reading a closely related book or text from the same topic area or viewing an appropriately selected related video resource. Thus, the same material and vocabulary are met and used through listening, speaking, reading, writing and viewing. This involves repeated encounters, receptive and productive retrieval, and receptive and productive varied use.

Retelling is another approach that supports learning and using vocabulary. After participating in the shared book activity, the teacher and the learners retell the text ideas or story (productive retrieval). This could first be retold together, followed by learners retelling more independently. Retelling is a powerful way to ensure comprehension has taken place, while creating an opportunity to retrieve, recall, reinforce and practise using words that are new, partially known or already learnt. If this is done as a class, with the teacher and learners engaging in rich conversation as they recall text ideas, retelling becomes a word-expanding, varied-use opportunity. This recall can be supported by the visuals in the book, and it is especially useful for retrieval if the text around or near the visuals is hidden. When the visuals are hidden, there is a higher cognitive load placed on the learners to recall, and remembering and use of words is pushed, ultimately resulting in greater learning potential.

Another possibility is to have a strong deliberate vocabulary attention element, getting the learners to recall the new words they met in the story. The teacher might provide context or visual clues to help this recall. Brief chats about a word or word group recalled enhances the value of the word's retrieval through deliberate elaboration. The teacher might also give additional information about the recalled words, such as other members of the word family, other related senses, and features of the spelling of the words.

When learners are beyond early reading stages, independent reading becomes a very powerful means of vocabulary growth. The number one goal of reading should be to get the learners reading successfully, in large quantities with enjoyment and comprehension.

We can look at the three types of reading from the viewpoint of the four strands. Most obviously, reading for fluency fits into the fluency development strand. Independent reading is largely meaning-focused input, but it has elements of language-focused learning when learners ask for the meaning of a word or consult a dictionary, and fluency development when the text becomes easier. Intensive reading is largely language-focused learning but can involve meaning-focused output when learners talk about the text.

Language use and language learning

Language use includes using the language receptively for listening and reading, and using the language productively for speaking and writing. Vocabulary and language use are related in two ways: vocabulary knowledge is needed for language use, and a learner's language use and potential to use language depend on vocabulary learning. The larger a learner's vocabulary, the more enabled they are to express their thinking verbally. Similarly, the more language use a learner is involved in—especially meaningful, engaging language at the boundary of the learner's knowledge—the more likely it is that their knowledge of vocabulary will grow. Let's look more closely at these two relationships.

Vocabulary knowledge supports language use

Research with learners of English as a foreign language suggests that 98% of the running words in a reading text need to be known if most learners are to gain adequate comprehension. Ninety-eight percent coverage means that only two words in 100, or one word in 50, is unknown. If we take the same text we looked at in Chapter 2, with 2% of the words unknown, it would look like this.

Box 7.1 A text marked to show the effect of not knowing a low density of low frequency words

The Travelling Musicians
An honest farmer had once an ass that had been a faithful servant to him a great many years, but was now growing old and every day more and more unfit for work. His master therefore was tired of keeping him and began to think of putting an end to him; but the ass, who saw that some mischief was in the wind, took himself YYYY off, and began his journey towards the great city, 'for there,' thought he, 'I may become a musician.'

After he had travelled a little way, he spied a dog lying by the roadside and panting as if he were tired. 'What makes you pant so, my friend?' said the ass. 'YYYY!' said the dog, 'My master was going to knock me on the head, because I am old and weak, and can no longer make myself useful to him in hunting; so I ran away; but what can I do to earn my YYYY?'

The text is 162 words long, so three words would be unknown at 98% coverage. The words replaced by YYYY (*slyly, alas, livelihood*) are the lowest-frequency words in the text. With this density of unknown words, the text is not too difficult to read. Research with native speakers suggests that 99% coverage may be a more suitable density, which would leave just one or two unknown words in the *Travelling Musicians* text. This is particularly so when the ideas, knowledge, topic content and themes of the text are new or outside the reader's current 'knowns'.

How large a vocabulary do you need to get 98% coverage of a text? It all depends on the kind of text. Table 7.4 provides figures for several different kinds of texts.

Table 7.4 English vocabulary sizes needed to get 95% and 98% coverage (including proper nouns) of various kinds of texts

Texts	95% coverage	98% coverage	Percentage of proper nouns in the texts
Novels	4,000 word families	9,000 word families	1-2%
Newspapers	4,000 word families	8,000 word families	5-6%
Children's movies	4,000 word families	6,000 word families	1.5%
Spoken English	3,000 word families	7,000 word families	1.3%
Books for beginning reading	3,000 word families	6,000 word families	2.8%
School Journals Part 1	3,000 word families	6,000 word families	2.6%

The figures in Table 7.4 slightly overestimate the vocabulary sizes needed for 95% and 98% coverage of children's texts because the lists used for the counting are based on adult collections of texts, and so among the high-frequency words are some that would not be known by young children. In addition, children know some words beyond the 6,000 level because of their special interests and because these words are used a lot in children's books and texts and not so often in other uses of the language. Nonetheless, young children in the first year or two of school would need a vocabulary size of around 3,000 words or so to cope with reading and understanding the written texts they have to read as they transition into becoming independent readers. Fortunately for most native-speaking children, they have large enough vocabulary sizes, and children's books are written to be easy for children to read.

Input supports vocabulary learning

Most of the vocabulary that native speakers know has been learned incidentally from input through language use when they are involved in quality and quantity talk-accompanied activities and reading. Every year, native speakers who are in high-quality and high-quantity talk and reading environments receive several million running words of input, and this contains words they know, words they partly know and words that are new to them. This input provides the opportunity to begin to learn new words, to strengthen and enrich knowledge of partly known words, and to become fluent in processing known words.

The incidental learning of a word is helped by multiple encounters with the word, especially when clues to the meanings of the words are available too. Multiple encounters are made more effective whenever (1) a learner is able to retrieve some previous knowledge of the word gained from previous meetings; (2) the word occurs in a new context; (3) the learner gives some deliberate attention to the word, such as by discussing the word with others, by looking it up in a dictionary or glossary, by noticing its similarity to other words through the word's shared parts, or by making an effort to remember it; and (4) when its meaning is clear from the text in which it occurs, including supportive pictures, photos or diagrams, or when it is clearly explained in the text.

Because multiple encounters are essential for learning, it is important that learners get large amounts of input. As learners' vocabulary size grows, they need increasingly greater amounts of input to get enough encounters with the words they next need to learn. As we saw in Chapter 2, words do not occur with equal frequency. So, in order to learn mid-frequency and low-frequency words, quite large amounts of input are needed.

Analysis of novels (Nation, 2014) and *School Journal*s suggests that young native speakers need to read for a reasonable amount of time each school day if they are to get enough opportunities to meet words a number of times over to add around 1,000 words a year to their vocabulary size through reading. The amount of reading done in the classroom complements their out-of-school reading, and vice versa. Table 7.5 suggests reading quantity goals for learners at different age levels. The calculations for these goals consider only opportunities for vocabulary learning and assume that learners aged 7 years are in the process of learning the fifth 1,000 word families, 8 years old the sixth 1,000 words, and so on.

Table 7.5 Recommended minimum amount of time to spend reading each school day for learners aged from 7 to 11 years

Age (years)	Minimum time to spend reading each school day
7	30 minutes per day
8	50 minutes per day
9	1 hour 10 minutes per day
10	1 hour 20 minutes per day
11	1 hour 30 minutes per day

These calculations are based on 40 weeks of the year and 5 days per week. The reading does not all need to be done in school time. If learners read on more days, such as weekends and during school breaks, the minimum amount of reading per day could be much shorter.

Table 7.5 looks only at reading, but input from spoken language also provides substantial opportunities for vocabulary learning. Although spoken language typically uses fewer different words, spoken language is not impoverished. Engaging in rich conversation as a class with the teacher as a prime scaffolder, meaningfully engaging with well-selected movie clips (now so readily available through the internet), engaging with other on-screen programmes that are high-quality and suitable for children, talking with a wide variety of people to broaden knowledge about how language is used, and listening to the radio all provide opportunities for vocabulary learning. The same helpful conditions of multiple encounters and clues to word meanings that occur in written text also occur when engaging with spoken language. While spoken language uses large numbers of high-frequency words more often than written language does, high-quality spoken text can be a powerful way to learn new words and consolidate the usage of words that are partially known.

For pre-school children, oral language is usually the only source of vocabulary learning. This learning is affected by the quantity and diversity of spoken language they hear, particularly language that is addressed directly to them and that engages them. Spoken language at school can also be an effective source of vocabulary knowledge. Deliberate attention to vocabulary learning through a multiplicity of ways, as already described in this book, should mean that learners' on-entry vocabulary gaps can gradually be minimised and the vocabulary knowledge of disadvantaged learners can make great strides in catching up to those more vocabulary advantaged.

When explicit attention is paid to expanding learners' vocabulary knowledge as an integral part of every school day, supported by home-based opportunities to grow their vocabulary, every learner stands to gain in vocabulary knowledge. Where this is fully embedded in every teacher's pedagogy across ages and stages, classes and subjects, every learner's vocabulary growth rate can accelerate (Farkas & Beron, 2004). Some schools and teachers are highly successful in exponentially accelerating every learner's vocabulary knowledge. Others are less successful. The difference is in the quantity and quality of attention given.

Implications for teaching and learning

1. A reading programme needs to include lots of independent reading, some shared or intensive reading, and reading of very easy material for fluency development.
2. A small number of conditions help vocabulary learning. Teachers need to remember and understand these conditions and make sure that some of them occur in all learner tasks and activities that have

the goal of vocabulary learning. Providing multiple encounters is by far the most important condition, and the other conditions constitute ways of increasing the quality of each re-encounter with a word.

3. Linked tasks, narrow reading, theme-related reading and re-reading are especially useful ways of providing opportunities to re-encounter words.

4. Learners need to read texts that are at the right level for them. This ensures they are not burdened by large amounts of unknown vocabulary and only have to deal with a low density of unknown words. Texts written for young native speakers generally meet this condition. These texts need to be supplemented by large amounts of engaging with texts that are rich in vocabulary and concepts, and offer varied text structure.

5. Learners need to do large quantities of reading in order to get multiple encounters of words to increase their vocabulary size. Teachers of young children need to make sure that a substantial part of each school day involves the learners doing reading of some kind or other. Teachers should also do what they can to encourage reading at home by providing books to read, by providing guidance for parents, and by motivating the learners.

6. Quality and quantity of talk in families and in classrooms, alongside other forms of extending spoken language, is an important means for vocabulary learning for learners in primary school, and beyond. Families need to understand the importance of quality and quantity of engaging talk with their children, and know how to engage in such conversations with their children. Teachers can support families in this endeavour (van Hees, 2000).

Further reading

For an example of vocabulary learning from listening to stories, see:

W. B. Elley. (1989). Vocabulary acquisition from listening to stories. *Reading Research Quarterly, 24*(2), 174–187.

For more about the various kinds of reading activities, see:

I. S. P. Nation. (2009). *Teaching ESL/EFL reading and writing.* New York, NY: Routledge.

For a detailed discussion of linked skills activities with plenty of examples, see Chapter 15 of:

P. Nation. (2013). *What should every ESL teacher know?* Seoul: Compass Publishing which is available free in an electronic form from the Compass Publishing website (http://www.compasspub.com/english/book/book_view.asp?h_seq=1721) and Paul Nation's website (http://www.victoria.ac.nz/lals/staff/paul-nation.aspx).

For more information on the vocabulary sizes needed to gain 98% coverage of various kinds of texts, see:

Carver, R. P. (1994). Percentage of unknown vocabulary words in text as a function of the relative difficulty of the text: Implications for instruction. *Journal of Reading Behavior, 26*(4), 413–437.

Macalister, J. (1999). School Journals and TESOL: An evaluation of the reading difficulty of School Journals for second and foreign language learners. *New Zealand Studies in Applied Linguistics, 5*, 61–85.

Nation, I. S. P. (2006). How large a vocabulary is needed for reading and listening? *Canadian Modern Language Review, 63*(1), 59–82.

Nation, I. S. P. (2014). How much input do you need to learn the most frequent 9,000 words? *Reading in a Foreign Language, 26*(2), 1–16.

van Hees, J. (2004). Partnerships at the interface: Classroom, whānau and community-based language and learning, for linguistically and culturally diverse learners. In *Language acquisition research* (pp. 81–113). Wellington: Research Division, Ministry of Education.

van Hees, J. (2007). *Expanding oral language in the classroom*. Wellington: NZCER.

Webb, S., & Macalister, J. (2013). Is text written for children useful for L2 extensive reading? *TESOL Quarterly, 47*(2), 300–322.

Webb, S., & Rodgers, M. P. H. (2009). The lexical coverage of movies. *Applied Linguistics, 30*(3), 407–427.

Webb, S., & Rodgers, M. P. H. (2009). The vocabulary demands of television programs. *Language Learning, 59*(2), 335–366.

For research on the vocabulary coverage needed for reading, see:

Hu, M., & Nation, I. S. P. (2000). Vocabulary density and reading comprehension. *Reading in a Foreign Language, 13*(1), 403–430.

Schmitt, N., Jiang, X., & Grabe, W. (2011). The percentage of words known in a text and reading comprehension. *The Modern Language Journal, 95*(1), 26–43.

For research on the quantity of reading needed and the times needed, see:

A. E. Cunningham. (2005). Vocabulary growth through independent reading and reading aloud to children. In E. H. Hiebert & M. L. Kamil (Eds.), *Teaching and learning vocabulary: Bringing research to practice* (pp. 45–68). Mahwah, NJ: Lawrence Erlbaum.

For research on shared reading, see

Evans, M. A., Williamson, K., & Pursoo, T. (2008). Preschoolers' attention to print during shared book reading. *Scientific Studies of Reading, 12*(1), 106–129.

Pollard-Durodola, S. D., Gonzalez, J. E., Simmons, D. C., Kwok, O., Taylor, A. B., Davis, M. J., ... & Simmons, L. (2011). The effects of an intensive shared book-reading intervention for preschool children at risk for vocabulary delay. *Exceptional Children, 77*(2), 161–183.

Chapter 8 **Teaching vocabulary**

Directly teaching vocabulary has been the focus of much research and debate. It is clear from studies of the vocabulary sizes of young native speakers and of the vocabulary sizes needed to read even beginning reading texts that teaching can only deal with a very small proportion of the words needed for reading.

Research on vocabulary teaching with young native speakers has shown that it can increase learners' oral vocabulary. The best effects come from a combination of deliberate teaching and incidental learning, and no special type of teaching stands out as being particularly effective. Paying attention to the optimal learning conditions should be at the core of any selected approach.

When we look closely at the efficiency of deliberate teaching in the research, however, the results are not encouraging. We can measure efficiency by seeing how many words were taught per hour and how many of these were actually learned. In several studies, on average, the teaching rate was one word per hour of instruction, and the learning rate was half that, at around one word learned every 2 hours. This is a ridiculously low learning rate, and teaching can be more efficient than that.

The important consideration when teaching vocabulary is that teaching be just one kind of deliberate attention and part of the language-focused learning strand. It needs to share time with the other three strands of meaning-focused input, meaning-focused output and fluency development. In other words, teaching can only be one small part of the opportunities for learning words, and it needs to be accompanied by a wide range of opportunities for incidental learning.

There are serious issues involved in the teaching of vocabulary to young native speakers.

1. Although there is a reasonably clear order in which words are learned and needed, research on vocabulary size shows that learners of the same age may be at different stages in their vocabulary growth. Words that learners with smaller vocabulary sizes need to learn will already be known by learners in the class who have larger vocabulary sizes. In addition, learners with the same vocabulary sizes do not know exactly the same words. It is fairly safe to say that any word at an appropriate level for one learner in a class is highly likely to be known by some other learners in the class. If we do not want to waste some learners' time, we need to individualize vocabulary teaching, or make sure the instruction is such that it will benefit all learners—those for whom it is a new word, those for whom it is a partly known word, and those who know it well. When learners are in multi-level groupings and input is pitched such that learners with greater or less vocabulary knowledge are alert to the potential to learn newly available words and share their known words with each other, there are many opportunities for vocabulary learning by each learner.

2. Closing the gap between young native speakers with average vocabulary sizes and those with smaller vocabulary sizes may require the learning of 500 to 2,000 word families. This number is in addition to the words that learners need to learn to maintain normal vocabulary growth. When this is broken down to words per school day, it is not such a formidable goal (around two to five additional words learned per day), but it requires sustained effort. One way of dealing with the gap is to set up a regular vocabulary teaching programme. Another way, and perhaps the most important, is to be attentive to ensuring rich spoken and written text is available throughout the teaching and learning of each school day. When these texts are engaged with by learners so they notice and discuss words as a natural part of their learning in the classroom, the gap can close quite dramatically.

3. A third and the most important way is to greatly increase the amount of reading and subject-related spoken language that

learners do. Incidental learning is not as effective as deliberate learning, but when there are large quantities of input, mileage and coverage can provide lots of opportunities for learning.

4. Another approach is to reconsider the learning goals. The minimum goal would be to make sure that the gap does not increase. A more ambitious goal would be to narrow the gap rather than close it. This is certainly a more realistic goal than closing the gap. If we could determine the minimum vocabulary sizes needed to deal successfully with the demands of spoken and written text at the various school year levels, these could be the goal. It remains to be seen whether these goals would be very different from average year level vocabulary sizes. Identifying year-level vocabulary sizes is no easy task nor likely to be a reliable indicator. What children know and need to know within curriculum and context learning is a moving target. Most research work in this area has been done in the United States. Because of this, direct transfer into other countries' educational systems may not be possible. Year levels in one country and what gets taught and is focused on at different stages and ages in primary schooling, may vary considerably.

5. Time spent on vocabulary teaching could be time taken away from engaging in potentially vocabulary-gifting talk, reading and subject-matter learning. One way of dealing with this is to make sure that the vocabulary teaching is directly related to the learning in hand—topics, subjects, and contexts. It does not make sense to have vocabulary teaching interventions, as are described in several published pieces of research, that occupy several hours a week and which achieve very low rates of actual learning. The time would be much better spent on increasing the amount of time spent engaging with Goldilocks zone oral language and reading texts.

As well as serious challenges, there are positive aspects to the teaching of vocabulary.

1. There is a rough order to learning, and this gives a band of at least 2,000 to 3,000 words to choose vocabulary from. Teachers can probably follow their intuitions once they know their learners' vocabulary sizes and are aware of the different levels of vocabulary. Appendix 1 in this book presents an activity to develop these intuitions.

2. Research shows that teaching does have positive effects on vocabulary knowledge and language use. Even a small amount of attention to a word or words can contribute to learning.

3. Teaching can help both those who have no knowledge of a particular word and those who have partial knowledge. It is likely that many more learners have partial knowledge than might be evident or than the tests show. This means there may be a wide band of learners in a class who may benefit in various ways from the teaching of any particular word or words.

4. Young learners have an immense capacity to learn many words at a fast pace when the context of learning is engaging and involving. It is important not to underestimate learners' capabilities. Be poised to 'gift' new or more words, knowing learners' potential to uptake and learn is often astounding. We can never know who learns and remembers and when they might do so, so err on being generous in making new words available.

5. Teaching can easily occur as part of subject-matter teaching and is likely to be more meaningful and memorable if it is related to particular content.

6. We know the learning conditions that favour vocabulary learning and teaching, even in fairly brief moments of vocabulary teaching. These are the conditions of recurring encounters, noticing, retrieval, varied use, elaboration and deliberate attention.

7. Depending on the quality of the program, digital learning can provide rich opportunities to learn new words, consolidate partially known words, and encounter words in engaging ways. Selecting high-quality digital programs is important. However, mesmerising digital vocabulary learning programs may well not result in a great deal of transferable vocabulary knowledge. Computer programs need to be chosen carefully and the ways of working with them carefully considered in light of the optimal conditions for learning.

Vocabulary teaching techniques

Let's now look at a range of useful ways of quickly directing learners' deliberate attention to words.

1. Quickly give *the meaning of the word* by:
   - using a simple explanation, either 'gifted' to the learners or quickly worked out together
   - thinking about known synonyms or 'like words'
   - giving a quick demonstration
   - drawing a simple picture or diagram
   - breaking the word into parts and giving the meaning of the parts and the whole word (the word part strategy)
   - giving several example sentences with the word in context to show the meaning—either 'gifting' these or working out ones together with the learners
   - commenting on the underlying meaning of the word and other things it refers to.
2. Draw attention to *the form of the word* by:
   - writing the word in some way—perhaps on the board so learners notice it
   - getting the learners to try out the pronunciation of the word several times
   - showing how the spelling of the word is like the spelling of known words
   - giving the stress pattern of the word and its pronunciation
   - showing the prefix, stem and suffix that make up the word
   - pointing out any spelling irregularities in the word.
3. Draw attention to *the use of the word* by:
   - Constructing sentences together and sharing known sentences that use the words in varied contexts and in well-constructed sentences; for example, the word *delightful*:
     a. It was *delightful* meeting up with my friend in the city and spending the whole afternoon with her.
     b. What a *delightful* smile your baby has.
     c. When children play together happily, it's *delightful* to watch.
   - quickly showing the grammatical pattern the word fits into (e.g. a qualifier in a noun group, as in b above—*a delightful smile*

- considering a few example collocates or words that typically occur with a particular word (e.g. *a delightful smile, a delightful day, it's delightful*)
- where applicable and appropriate, mentioning any restrictions on the use of the word (formal, colloquial, impolite, only used in American English or British English, only used with children, old-fashioned, technical, infrequent)
- considering commonly used synonyms (like-words) and opposites (e.g. *delightful*—enchanting, attractive, happy-making; disappointing, unattractive, off-putting).

There are several principles to guide ways of quickly giving attention.

1. Keep the teaching simple and clear. Don't use complicated explanations—comprehensible, short and precise is best.
2. Relate the current learning to previous learning, and be alert to the transferability of the new learning into other contexts and texts.
3. Use oral, visual and written modes that complement each other.
4. Give the most attention to words that are already partly known.
5. Don't bring in other unknown or poorly known related words, like near synonyms, opposites, or members of the same lexical set (a group of same topic words). This sets up confusion.

These are the main ways teachers should give attention to particular words. In the long run they are much more efficient and effective than more elaborate vocabulary teaching activities.

Vocabulary learning exercises that require little or no preparation

Let's now look at a range of vocabulary activities that require very little preparation by the teacher but that spend a little more time on each word. Note that these activities have been organised according to the three main aspects of what is involved in knowing a word, as shown in Table 3.1. Many of these activities involve learners working together in pairs or small groups and collaboratively with the teacher.

Box 8.1 Exercises that require little or no preparation

Word meaning	
Find the core meaning	Working with the teacher or in pairs: depending on age and stage, the learners talk about the possible meaning of the word or words. Talking about possible meanings before looking up the word in the dictionary enhances remembering when looked up. Learners then look at dictionary entries in several dictionaries and find the shared meaning in the various senses of the word. There is a 'word expert' template to guide learners with this in Appendix 9.
Word card testing	The learners work in pairs. They have a pack of cards, each one with a word on the front and the meaning on the back. Each learner gives their pack of cards to their partner, who tests them on their recall of the meaning by saying the word and getting them to give the meaning. This can also be done by giving the meaning and getting them to recall the word form.
Dictionary use	When a useful word occurs in a reading or oral text, the teacher trains learners to try to explain or give a meaning for the word, followed up by a quick dictionary search.
Guessing from context	Whenever a guessable word occurs in a reading text, the teacher trains the learners in the guessing-from-context strategy.
Word form	
Spelling dictation	The teacher says words or phrases and the learners write them. The learners then check what they have written against each other's efforts and a model. This can be used even with young learners who are beginner writers.
Pronunciation	The teacher writes up words on the board or in a place clearly seen and the learners pronounce them, getting feedback from the teacher. Each learner picks which word to say from the list on the board.
Word parts	The teacher writes words and the learners break them into parts and give the meanings of the parts. This needs to be guided and modelled by the teacher initially, but there may be much over time the learners can do without direct assistance from the teacher. Trying is important. Examples: **suggestion** = *suggest – give a number of options or possibilities or ideas; -tion – the act of suggesting.* *traffic jam = traffic – vehicles or people moving along; jam – pushed together.*
Word use	
Suggest collocates	The learners work together in pairs or small groups to list collocates for a given word (other words the target word often or usually occurs with).
Word experts	A learner reports on a word he or she has found in their reading or heard. They talk about the meaning, spelling, pronunciation, word parts, etymology (word history), collocates and grammar of the word, sharing with other learners. A teacher can be a model for this and participate regularly to expand the focus of attention. Of course, for young learners, the teacher will need to lead the way and select only that which the learners can adequately cope with.

The words for these activities can be chosen during classroom learning. It could be that one learner or several learners as a team (class recorders) have the job of noting words for future reference and attention. For young learners the teacher or learning assistant may need to do this. Alternatively, the teacher may choose words that have appeared in work over the previous days, or words the learners need to know from the mid-frequency words, and record these in some way for learners to engage with further. A word wall is ideal for this.

Ensuring words are encountered many times

Multiple encounters with words is the most important condition for vocabulary learning, and so teachers should have ways of making sure target words are encountered more than once by learners. There are many ways this can be done. Here are some examples.

1. Have each learner attend to a word on their own, followed by sharing in a pair, followed by whole-class sharing. In this way the word has been noticed and worked with a number of times.

2. Word expert (see Appendix 9) has learners considering the word in focus in multiple ways so that they re-encounter the word a number of times.

3. Put words that have already been given attention onto a class interactive word wall. When word wall pieces fit together in several ways, there are many ways they can be made into learning games so that the words are focused on many times over.

4. Put words into a vocabulary box or bag for choosing and sorting. In the same or different boxes there could be cards with a word's meaning and the word used in context sentences. A word card or a meaning card or a word context card is chosen from a box, and matching cards from the other boxes are located and talked about, and read. Each time a word is a word that has been given attention again, the matched cards could either be put back into the box with the rest, or pulled out to avoid the same ones being chosen.

5. Get learners to play the game of pointing out when previously met words occur again throughout class learning. Often learners will do this spontaneously.

Because so many words need to be given deliberate attention during a year (several hundred at least), it is not worth keeping a list of the words. At most, the teacher could print out a list of the fourth 1,000 words, for example, and together with the learners tick them as attention to them occurs. As words receive attention throughout a term, the words that have cropped up and received specific attention could be bagged or accumulated into a large book with an appropriate title. The most useful re-encountering of words paid attention to during deliberate teaching will be when the learners meet the words again because there is ongoing inclusion of word-rich texts throughout a school day.

Providing vocabulary support for reading

Pre-teaching

Research does not strongly support the pre-teaching of vocabulary before learners deal with the text in which they occur, particularly when comprehension of the text is the goal. The best way to pre-teach vocabulary is to make it part of stimulating discussion about the topic to be considered in the book or the text to be heard, drawing on learners' current knowledge, enhanced by elaborative talk by the teacher and each other.

Stimulating talk about the topic prior to reading or further deep work with a spoken text, and pre-teaching vocabulary, has two different effects on reading a text or more fully understanding a spoken text of some kind. Stimulating learners' knowledge about the topic makes it easier for learners to understand the major ideas and contents of a text. Pre-teaching vocabulary helps learners understand particular parts of the text to come; for example, the word in a word group, or the word group itself, or in a sentence or expanded utterance.

Pre-teaching as part of stimulating learners' current knowledge puts the vocabulary in helpful contexts and makes sure the vocabulary really is relevant for the reading or spoken text that follows. It also allows the teacher to see if learners already know the words or if the words require some attention. When learners read the text or hear the spoken text, pre-attention provides conditions for noticing and attending to the vocabulary when used in the text itself. Thus, learning potential is heightened.

If the reading or spoken text is an important one for the learners, you need to make sure that most time is spent on the text and not on pre-teaching and stimulating learners' current knowledge and perspectives. Time on this needs to be brief, so that the most time is spent on the text itself.

Dealing with vocabulary while reading
The principle guiding intensive reading is that work on today's text should, over time, build more learner capability to handle the following texts. From a vocabulary perspective, this means focusing on vocabulary that is likely to occur again and words that are important meaning-carrying words to comprehend the text. Focusing on vocabulary strategies such as guessing from context, using word parts, and dictionary use are useful supports, as are quick, short discussions about words.

Theme-based learning is particularly helpful for vocabulary learning because it means that theme-related vocabulary keeps coming back again and again, and this re-encountering helps vocabulary learning potential. It also means the vocabulary is likely to recur in contexts of varied use. Unless the word is central to the whole reading or spoken text, quickly giving attention to the word, as described in the section in this chapter on vocabulary teaching and learning techniques. Giving attention to the meaning should be the first choice, and this can be accompanied by brief attention to the form or use of the word.

Interference
When teaching vocabulary it is very tempting to bring together a group of related words—such as the names of animals, or fruit, or trees—and teach them together. Groups of words like these are called lexical sets. The research on teaching lexical sets is surprising, but convincing, because this is one of the few areas of applied linguistics where the same experiments have been repeated several times to see if the results agree. The findings are that teaching items in lexical sets makes learning 50 to 100% *more difficult*. That is, more recurrences of the word are needed to make words in lexical sets stick in memory than when learning in a text context or when not organised into related sets. The reason encountering words in a lexical set is likely to cause confusion or low learning is because the items in a set interfere with each other. For example, when learning the points of the compass, we not only have to learn *north*, *east*, *south* and *west*, but we also have to stop them

getting mixed up with each other. The same learning difficulty occurs with opposites and near synonyms. For example, if both *amateur* and *professional* are unknown, learning them both at the same time makes the learning much more difficult.

However, when learners have already built up some knowledge of related words, paying attention to two words like *amateur* and *professional* by talk and discussion can lead to clarification and realisation, and create a great deal of interest in the words. When learners are fairly new to English, learning both words may put too heavy a learning burden on them.

The good news is that words that are related to each other in the form of a story or within a text, like *escape, jungle, conceal* and *fog*, are learned more easily together than unrelated words. The same is probably true of words that could be part of a factual account or description. The rough guide is that if items can be put into a list, like the names of flowers or articles of furniture, they are likely to be more difficult to learn together. If they can be put together to make a sentence or a connected piece of text or an account, then they are likely to be learned more easily at the same time.

Interference occurs when words that are unknown or poorly known are learned at the same time. However, when all the words are known or only one or two are unknown, it is a good idea to bring them together to see their subtle differences. WordPlosion (Chapter 11) is an example where associated words do not cause confusion. Rather, they enhance knowing the target word.

Analysing deliberate learning activities

The success of deliberate vocabulary learning and incidentally learning vocabulary depends on the learning conditions when these words occur. These learning conditions are covered by three very important general principles:

1. We learn what we focus on (the focus principle).
2. The deeper the quality of attention we give to an item, the more likely it is to be remembered (the depth-of-processing principle).
3. The more often we meet an item, the more likely we are to learn it (the recycling or re-encountering principle).

These principles are closely related to each other. If recycling involves depth of processing, and this processing involves a focus on important aspects of the word involving its form, meaning or use, the more likely the word is to be learned.

Teachers need to understand these principles and know how to apply them across a balanced range of activities.

When looking at a task or learning context, the teacher needs to consider what aspect of vocabulary knowledge (form, meaning or use) is being focused on, what conditions are likely to occur that provide depth of processing, and what opportunities for recycling are factored in. As we saw in Chapter 5 (on learning conditions), there are five major conditions: noticing, retrieval, varied use, elaboration, and deliberate attention. These are listed in order of depth, with elaboration and deliberate attention being the deepest. The condition of engagement with the topic and with the activity affects all the other conditions.

Let's now look at how these conditions apply to commonly used teacher-led or teacher-guided *class discussion*, with the teacher and learners interacting on a particular topic.

Class discussion

The worst way of running a class discussion is for the teacher to ask a series of questions, with one learner answering when the teacher chooses them to answer. This way involves minimal recycling, minimises the chances for each learner to be actively involved, and limits the learners' initiative to explore the topic or point of discussion further together, with the teacher as a key scaffolding participant.

How class discussion can be done optimally is fully explored and explained in van Hees's book, *Expanding Oral Language in the Classroom* (van Hees, 2007). Each and every learner thinking, sharing ideas and considering the contributions of others in order to respond out loud or simply think about is at the heart of useful class discussion.

Who gets to share can be decided in various ways (see van Hees, 2007):

1. Write the names of all the group or class on ice-block sticks, place them in a tin, and pull out a stick to identify a learner to share.
2. Randomly select a learner simply by roving around the group in no particular order, with no hands up by learners.

These two ways are good because each learner knows they are a potential sayer and contributor, which means they notice and prepare more consciously, and are more likely to pay attention to what gets contributed.

Another way is simply to have the learners self-select, with contributions made in a conversational manner within a culture of 'we all share and take turns'. By discussing with learners the benefits of contributing, they are aware of and become self-advocates for their own and others' learning under good learning conditions. As well as providing more opportunity for learners to explore the topic and to compare their ideas with others, this way of doing the activity provides more opportunities for recycling of the target vocabulary, for productive and varied use of the vocabulary, and for maximising engagement and noticing.

Dictionary use is a dominant activity promoted in classrooms. For immediate clarification, consulting a dictionary may prove useful, but for strengthened learning of an unknown word learners should engage in pair and group discussion about the word's meaning and examine its use in context before looking it up in a dictionary.

Let's now look at a range of useful vocabulary-focused classroom activities to see how they work and how they are best used.

Intensive reading

Intensive reading has many names. The activity involves the teacher and learners working through a text together to gain a deep and thoughtful understanding of the text. The activity can last for around 20 to 40 minutes, making use of a short text that is not too difficult to read but provides an opportunity to explore important text ideas and the vocabulary associated with these. The students can sit in pairs for ease of discussion, with one copy of the text between them. Ensuring both learners see the text equally well and take turns, and share together throughout, is important.

The first step is to explain the purpose of what is to come and introduce the story in some way. Invite the learners to share their current knowledge and experiences related to the topic in hand. This is important and should not be omitted. Connecting known knowledge to new helps learning.

At this point, consider touching on some of the important things in the text to come. This might include looking at the title and talking about it. If there are visuals such as photos, drawings or diagrams, viewing these and talking about them is useful and helps open up the meaning that might be in the written text. It also offers an opportunity to pre-teach a few very important words. The pre-teaching should include saying the words, understanding their meaning, talking about and using them in context sentences, and looking at their printed form.

A second step is to get the learners to quietly read the story by themselves or together in pairs. If more support is needed, have them follow the story as you read the text, using a shared-book approach.

Next, you and the learners work their way through the story, discussing the ideas in small text chunks and making sure the story and its implications are well understood. This discussion provides an opportunity for focusing on words and word groups, and for clarifying their meaning through rewording and examples.

A final step involves you and the learners recalling ideas in the story, perhaps retelling the text in their own words if it is a narrative, and discussing the main idea or overall theme.

Talk-accompanied shared reading like this provides excellent opportunities for the conditions of noticing, quality of attention, and recycling. While working through the text there can be a deliberate focus on words and word groups. This focus can involve thoughtful attention by relating text ideas to the learners' known experiences and knowledge. The vocabulary in the text is put into new contexts through the discussion, and this varied use of the vocabulary makes a strong contribution to learning. The four steps of this reading approach (introduction, reading, discussion, recalling) provide excellent opportunities for recycling. We look at intensive reading again in Chapter 10.

Collective gifting and sharing

Prepare a set of visuals related to a specific topic. Topic examples include bullying, electricity, pollution, the weather, or cars. The visuals can include pictures, objects and diagrams. First, introduce the topic while showing the visuals. The learners can also contribute what they know about the topic. Next, each learner individually writes down words and phrases connected to the topic. Then in pairs each learner shares their list with their partner, explaining the connection to the topic and dealing with any comments or challenges by their partner. At the same time, write down a list of words and phrases associated with the topic, with each word or phrase on a different slip of paper. The learners should check each other's work for accurate spelling.

Next, the learners work as a whole class and each pair suggests a word or phrase for the others to consider. The class discuss the relevance of the word or phrase to the topic, and if they are generally happy with it they underline it on their own list if they already have it there, or they add it to their own list.

Finally, share your list with the class, holding up the slip of paper containing the word or phrase. If the word or phrase is on the students' lists, they circle it on their list, and if not, they add it to their list. As each word or phrase is shown, the learners discuss its relevance to the topic.

This activity can be a useful introduction to further work on the topic, or it can be used as a way of recycling and expanding on vocabulary related to a topic that has been covered a few weeks before. It can also be followed up with a classifying procedure, where the vocabulary is organised into groups according to the parts of the topic.

The activity is called a *pyramid procedure* because the work moves down a widening pyramid, starting with individual activity, then moving to pair activity, and then moving to whole-class activity focusing on the same material. The activity provides enormous amounts of recycling, and elaboration of vocabulary items through discussion of their relevance to the topic. It is worthwhile monitoring the discussion to see how the vocabulary is used or focused on during the discussion; that is, how much noticing, retrieval, varied use, elaboration and deliberate attention are involved. See a detailed description in van Hees (2014).

Word wall

The word wall is a way to collect words for further deliberate attention. The word wall can be presented in various ways, but in most cases both the meanings and the forms of the words are provided. These can be complemented by word usage: the word is used in one or two contextually appropriate sentences. A suggested approach follows (van Hees, 2001).

Write the word on a piece of card and its meaning on a different-coloured card. The contextual sentences may be on a different coloured card again. The words are pinned on to the wall, with their meanings and contextual sentences pinned separately so that they can be removed or moved. Words should come from one of three main sources and are arranged on the word wall according to either focus or source, as follows:

- words arising throughout the day—ones that 'crop up'
- words that come from texts the learners have been reading, or topics they have been studying
- words derived from specific phonological focuses (e.g. blends, prefixes, suffixes).

Ideally, most of the words on the word wall should be from the vocabulary frequency levels just beyond the learners' present vocabulary size: either previously unknown words or words only partially known.

For many students, knowing a word is more strongly receptive than productive. To consolidate and expand the learner's word knowledge, when words understood or partially known are given attention, the learner's receptive knowledge is pushed towards greater fullness of knowing the word, including productive knowledge.

The word wall can be used to help vocabulary learning in the following ways.

- The meanings are taken off the wall, shuffled, and learners have to match the words and their meanings.
- The meanings are taken off the wall, and the learners are asked to recall the meanings when the words are pointed to.
- The word forms are taken off the wall, and the learners are asked to recall and spell the words.
- The teacher and students explore more about some of the words in order to show their range of uses.

Phonologically derived words might be ones identified when there is a blend in focus; for example, the *bl-* blend. The learners, with support from the teacher, might identify a list of words with this blend: *black, blister, blow, blame, blanket, blood, blind, blue*. Along with a focus on the blend, the words are considered for meaning and contextual use.

Similarly, high-frequency words appropriate to the age and stage of the learners can be part of the word wall, so that not only is there a focus on automaticity in saying, reading and writing the word, but the words are considered for meaning and contextual use.

The main learning condition provided by the word wall is deliberate attention. This deliberate attention can be deepened by providing chances for retrieval by getting learners to recall the meanings of the words, by seeing the meanings and getting learners to recall the form of the words, and by relating the words to previous meetings in use or to future applications. The words on the word wall can also become the focus of analysis of word parts or sound–spelling combinations, which set up the condition of elaboration.

Semantic mapping
Semantic maps go by many names (word maps, mind maps, concept diagrams, concept maps) and involve the teacher working with the learners to build up a map of ideas and words associated with a particular topic or concept. A word or word group capturing the topic is placed at the centre of the map, and aspects of the topic are organised and expanded on through discussion. Evolving ideas are drawn into a semantic map by relating and connecting the ideas. Particular attention is given to explaining and linking the various aspects of the topic, and clarifying the vocabulary related to those aspects. This kind of discussion is the essence of semantic mapping.

Semantic mapping has two main goals: (a) content matter learning, including triggering learners' current knowledge, thinking and experiences; and (b) vocabulary expansion. Some versions of semantic mapping involve the teacher providing prepared ideas and vocabulary related to the topic, and then through discussion in pairs, and later as a class group perhaps, organising the vocabulary into one or more semantic maps. Semantic maps have no fixed organisational outcome but can be constructed variously depending on the thinking and perspective of the constructors. This makes them particularly valuable for affirming the individuality of learners.

Semantic mapping can be used to revise a topic the learners have recently studied or know much about. It encourages retrieval of current and previously met vocabulary. Semantic mapping can also be based on a recent event, or on shared cultural knowledge, and can be used to introduce a topic by capturing what learners already know and perceive about a topic. There are many possibilities for where to go after semantic mapping. The important point is that focused attention is given to words and their meanings when learners are involved in semantic mapping. There is usually much talk and discussion about where to place and align ideas and vocabulary, and in this way attention is enhanced.

In many ways it is the interaction and quality of talk that are important in the co-construction of knowledge between the teacher and learners, and between learners.

Learning from semantic mapping is heavily dependent on how the steps and processes are managed and proceed. Deliberate attention given to explaining and noticing form as part of constructing a semantic map by and with learners, using both spoken and written modes, needs to be staged in an integrated way. Spoken and written attention to words arising or provided should occur together throughout.

For example, at the initial scoping stage learners and the teacher might work together to generate ideas and words, or these might have been previously prepared by the teacher. In both situations, discussion and recording or reading and discussion happen together. In terms of vocabulary learning, the co-occurring modes of speaking and listening, reading and recording, heighten the attention and noticing given to ideas and words.

At times learners may work in pairs, independent of the teacher; at other times it may be larger group sharing. How steps play out will depend on the age and stage of the learners, the extent of their English language and content knowledge and capability, and the group dynamics specific to the context. Suggested steps for semantic mapping with learners are provided in Appendix 6 (van Hees, 2001).

Semantic mapping includes much recycling of vocabulary. Discussion about words or ideas to include offers one layer of recycling. Justifying their placement when discussing within and across pairs, groups or when co-constructing a class semantic map, again recycles the words many times over. Varied use is also part of this. Semantic mapping strongly sets up the learning conditions of elaboration and deliberate attention.

It is important to choose prepared words for semantic mapping carefully, in the Goldilocks zone of the learners: not too many, not too few; not too complex, not too simple. When a semantic map is generated by learners and teacher together, on the spot, deciding on what to include and what not to include from contributions made by learners needs to be carefully handled. The Goldilocks zone principle applies here too. On the one hand, learners' contributions need to be included and validated, but some culling and selection may be necessary.

Semantic mapping helps develop learners' word consciousness, an important aspect of the process and steps. Word consciousness is the focus of the next chapter.

Implications for teaching and learning

1. Teachers should direct deliberate attention to words that are likely to be unknown or partly known. This attention need not involve spending a lot of time on each word, but should be enough to make a small step forward in knowing the word.
2. Where possible, drawing attention to vocabulary should involve retrieval, varied use and elaboration.
3. Teachers need to find ways of coming back to words that have already been taught, so that the words get plenty of recycled noticing and attention.
4. Recycling words should move learners from handling them receptively towards productive use.
5. Teachers need to develop an awareness of which words are mid-frequency or Goldilocks-zone words and direct learners' attention towards them. Ideally, this should be done not as a separate vocabulary learning session but as part of day-to-day curriculum teaching and learning.

Further reading

For a survey of studies of the effects of teaching vocabulary to young native speakers, see:

L. M. Marulis, & S. B. Neuman. (2010). The effects of vocabulary intervention on young children's word learning: A meta-analysis. *Review of Educational Research, 80*(3), 300–335.

For more on vocabulary teaching, see Chapter 7 of:

I. S. P. Nation. (2008). *Teaching vocabulary: Strategies and techniques*. Boston, MA: Heinle Cengage Learning.

For more on a vocabulary box, see:

A. Coxhead. (2004). Using a class vocabulary box: How, why, when, where and who. *Guidelines*, *26*(2), 19–23.

For research on the effects of background knowledge and vocabulary on reading, see:

S. A. Stahl, V. C. Hare, R. Sinatra, & J. F. Gregory. (1991). Defining the role of prior knowledge and vocabulary in reading comprehension: The retiring of number 41. *Journal of Reading Behavior*, *23*(4), 487–508.

For a summary of the research on interference between members of the same lexical set, see:

I. S. P. Nation. (2000). Learning vocabulary in lexical sets: Dangers and guidelines. *TESOL Journal*, *9*(2), 6–10.

For a discussion of semantic mapping see:

S. A. Stahl, & S. J. Vancil. (1986). Discussion is what makes semantic maps work in vocabulary instruction. *The Reading Teacher*, *40*(1), 62–67.

Chapter 9 Word consciousness

Imagine a classroom where learners are excited about meeting new words, where they bring words they have met outside class to explain to their classmates, where they immediately look at breaking an unfamiliar word into parts and connecting it with other related words they know, where they know where to go to find out what a word means, and where they have a well-practised system for making a note of the word and making sure it will be remembered. Such a classroom is one where the teacher has the goal of developing learners' *word consciousness*.

Word consciousness involves learners becoming consciously aware of words, their nature and the jobs they do. This consciousness can include becoming aware of word parts (prefixes, suffixes and stems) and word families, becoming aware of core meanings and the various senses of words, becoming aware of homographs, homophones and homonyms, knowing ways to find out more about words by putting effort into trying to work out word meanings and consulting dictionaries or other sources, developing an awareness that words have histories (etymology), and becoming aware of how the choice of words affects the message of a text. Children are fascinated with words and seem naturally to note and enquire about the known, partly known and unknown words they encounter. Even young learners can be fascinated by seeing how a program like the Frequency program at http://www.lextutor.ca can turn a text into a frequency list, and how the frequencies of words are very different from each other.

Word consciousness should involve an excitement and interest in words that is not limited to a particular subject or part of the day but runs through all subjects and extends outside the classroom and school day. The goals of word consciousness are to:

- encourage deliberate attention to words (a powerful learning condition)
- develop a curiosity and interest in vocabulary and vocabulary learning
- make the learning of vocabulary easier by being aware of the systems that lie behind words and their use.

Word consciousness can be developed by a range of strategies, usually initially introduced by the teacher, but as a word conscious culture develops among the learners they can and will take over control of these strategies, becoming increasingly more word conscious.

This chapter contains 12 different focuses, with several examples that are ready to use. Table 3.1 in Chapter 3, which lists the various aspects of what is involved in knowing a word, contains some of the features that can be a focus for word consciousness. This chapter could be organised around the three headings of those aspects: form (see 3, 4, 9, 12 below), meaning (see 1, 2, 7 below) and use (see 5, 6, 8, 10, 11 below), but is arranged so that the most useful and effective word consciousness activities come first.

Word consciousness focus activities

1. Word senses

Description
A word can be used in many ways, but although it has many different uses it usually has the same meaning running through the different uses. This is called its core meaning. For example, we can use the word *foot* to talk about *the foot of a hill, the foot of a tree, the foot of the bed, a footnote*, and, of course, *a sore foot*. These all share the core meaning of being at the bottom.

Example activity
Look at the different senses of each of these two words and say what is the same about them. (For example, what is similar between *peel an apple* and *peeled off his clothes*?)

Table 9.1 Two words with a range of senses

Sweet	Peel
Sweet taste	Peel an apple
Sweet music	Peeled off his clothes
Sweet face	The paint is peeling.
Sweet as!	He peeled off from the group.
You are very sweet.	An orange peel

Answers: *sweet* = nice, attractive; *peel* = remove the outside from the main part

Look at the different senses of each of these two words and say what is the same about them.

Table 9.2 Find the core meaning in these words

Run	Shallow
Run away	A shallow river
Running water	In the shallows
A runny nose	A shallow person
The movie runs for two hours.	A shallow cut

Answers: *run* = move continuously; *shallow* = not deep

Justification for the word senses activity

It is easier to learn words which share the underlying meaning of the stem word in some way. Learners can quickly grow an expanded word knowledge related to the word. The less concrete or more unusual use of the word still carrying the underlying meaning in some way, 'stretches' the core word's meaning, as in the example above.

Some people think that different senses are different meanings, making these different uses into different words. However, learners meet different senses of words all the time and are usually able to deal with them with the help of context. Occasionally they may meet a use that puzzles them. Looking for the core meaning of a word is one way of dealing with this. When learners are able to use dictionaries, dictionary entries can be used for this activity. For example, "Look up the word *neutral* in the dictionary. How many senses does it have? Are they all drawing on the same core meaning?"

Teachers also need to realise that different senses of words do not need to be taught as if they were different words. Knowing a word's core underlying meaning allows learners to make informed guesses at different senses of the word. When drawing attention to an unfamiliar sense, it is important to show how it contains the same core meaning shared by the other senses.

Discussion and writing meanings (definitions or explanations) can be used as a part of this consciousness-raising focus. The learners might work in pairs or groups of three to explain a word and shape up a clear, succinct and precise definition of it to cover most of its uses. If several pairs or small groups work on the same word, they can then compare and discuss their explanations and definitions with more or less teacher support. A consensus definition can go up on the word wall. This approach has the aim of not only deepening understanding of a particular word, but also developing an awareness that core meanings are typically more general than any one of their senses, particularly their most concrete use.

2. Using a dictionary

Description

Learners need to be quite good at reading before they can use a dictionary. There are, however, dictionaries specially designed for young children. It is a good idea to encourage learners to have a guess at the meaning of a word using contextual clues before they look up a word. Because dictionary entries have several senses for a word, it is useful to practise finding the most appropriate sense. It is also worth viewing a full dictionary entry and discussing its parts. The way dictionaries are made varies, and this is helpful and interesting for learners to know about.

Activity

Here is one approach to help learners gain awareness of the parts of a dictionary entry. The approach requires a level of learner independence whereby they are able to work together in groups without a great deal of guidance by the teacher.

Divide learners into groups ranging from four to six. (With younger learners, working in pairs is best.) Give each person a short sentence on a strip of paper about how dictionary entries commonly provide information about a word. Each learner reads, understands and memorises their sentence strip. Collect these up. Each learner then has to say their sentence to the other learners, either in their group or when learners come together as a class group. In the eight-person group format the learners decide on the right order as is commonly used in dictionaries, simply by listening to all the sentences, each memorised by one learner.

It may be necessary to model the negotiation that will need to go on, which will probably include a number of 'saying rounds'. No writing is allowed. When the group thinks they have all of them in order, the class comes together to share and discuss, with dictionaries on hand to check their decisions.

If learners are in groups of four or in pairs, a slightly adjusted approach will need to be used. However, whether with more or less independence, with larger or small learner groups, the learners gain simply by processing the strips, and trying to understand the meaning and what occurs in sequence in a dictionary entry. Attention, noticing, retrieval and recycling all come into play.

The suggested sentences are:

a. The pronunciation of the word is given.
b. Next, the entry gives the part of speech of the word.
c. The meaning of the word is the next part of the dictionary entry.
d. The entry may then show a sentence using the word.
e. The entry for each word part has its parts arranged in a certain order.
f. The spelling of the word is the first part of the entry.
g. The related forms of the word are then shown.
h. Then the entry may show different spellings of the word.

(A possible correct order is e, f, h, a, b, g, c, d, but different dictionaries may have a slightly different order and may have more or less information about each word.)

The teacher can add sentences to this list or take them away so that they match the information in the dictionaries the learners typically use. Other sentences could include: 'The entry may show different pronunciations for the word', 'The origin of the word is given' and 'Then the entry provides information about the grammar of the word'.

The typical practice is to get the learners to look up the meanings of words. For example, use a dictionary to look up the meaning of these words: *awash, sandal, somewhat, gracious, sandwich, tow, lonely*. (Word choices will depend on learners' age and stage.) There are many skills involved in simply looking up one of these words—alphabet knowledge, initial and later position in a word, understanding the entry information, deciding on a meaning that fits the word in contexts, and reading the entry. Dictionaries designed for young learners or newer learners of English often have fewer and simpler entries for this reason. This is both helpful and limiting, as words arising that learners may attempt to look up may well not be in the dictionary. The teacher will need to decide how much guidance is needed, how much can be done independently, and how much needs to be done collaboratively as a class group.

Looking up words in a dictionary assumes knowing how to spell the word. If the word to look up is only available orally, then learners often grapple with its spelling and flounder trying to locate the word as an entry in the dictionary. Attempts to overcome this limitation have been made by developers of the poor spellers dictionary. While in principle the idea is good, in practice looking up a word in a poor spellers dictionary is also laced with limitations. For example, if the word heard is *subtle*, the poor speller may try to look up any number of spelling attempts, such as *suttel*, *sutle*, or *suttill*. It may well be that none of these spelling attempts are available in the dictionary entries. Trialing the poor spellers dictionary with some learners, van Hees found the learners were no better off overall in terms of being able to look up words than with a normal dictionary. The best approach seems to be for learners to attempt to spell the word before looking it up, and if they feel unsure, to ask someone to write the word for them.

Justification for the using a dictionary activity
When learners can use a dictionary, they increase their independence in learning about words, especially their meanings. It is this independence that makes this focus of consciousness-raising an important focus. High-quality electronic dictionaries are now readily available, even on cellphones, and learners can learn to use them as a quick access resource about words.

3. Word families, and prefixes and suffixes

Description

A word family is a group of words that all share the same word stem but differ from each other by having different prefixes and/or suffixes. For example, here is the word family for *hurry*:

>hurried
>hurriedly
>hurries
>hurrying
>unhurried
>unhurriedly

Notice how some words have both a prefix and a suffix, and how it is possible for a word to have more than one suffix. It is also possible for a word to have more than one prefix. For example, *unmistaken*, has the prefixes *un-* and *mis-*.

There are two kinds of word stems: those that are words by themselves without any prefix or suffix (such as *hurry*), and those that must have a prefix or suffix and cannot be used with the same meaning by themselves; for example *spect* as in *spectacles, inspect, respect*. Stems that can be a word by themselves are called free stems. Stems that need a prefix or suffix are called bound stems. Appendix 7 has a list of the most common bound stems.

Activity

Here are some useful activities with word parts. You can use these with your learners at an appropriate age and stage using the words listed below. One list has higher-frequency words, the other has words in the mid-frequency range.

Get learners to sort words into families. What endings do the different family members have (suffixes)? Can members of the same word family have different beginnings (prefixes)? The same words can also be used for practising breaking words into prefixes, suffixes and stems. In the two following boxes the headword for each family is on the first row.

Table 9.3a A list of high-frequency words for sorting into families

run	kind	shape	safe
shapely	unsafely	reshaping	rerun
unkind	runner	unshapely	reshape
running	shaped	kindliness	unkindly
unkindliness	kindly	rerunning	shaping
unsafely	unkind	unsafe	safely

Table 9.3b A list of mid-frequency words for word part analysis

adequate	adjusting	readjustment	inadequately
adjustable	adjustment	cycling	defeats
cycled	defeatist	readjusted	inadequate
adequately	adjustments	cyclist	nonadjustable
adjust	cycle	defeatism	readjust
defeating	readjustments	unadjusted	adjusts
adjusted	cycles	defeat	readjusting
cyclists	adjusters	cyclic	readjusts
adjuster	cyclical	defeated	undefeated

Learners should deliberately learn the forms and meanings of the most useful prefixes. The following lists (Table 9.4) are the most useful starting point. Begin with the first list. Note how some prefixes change their ending to agree with the beginning of the stem (*in-*, for example, can be *in-*, *im-*, *ir-*, *il-*).

Table 9.4 Two lists of useful prefixes for learning

List 1		
Prefix	Meaning	Example words
ex	former	ex-president, ex-wife
mis	wrongly	misfit, misinform, misspeak
semi	half	semi-automatic, semicircle
inter	between, among	inter-African; interweave
mid	middle	mid-week, midway
un-	not	unable, unworried
non-	not	non-violent, non-cooperative
sub	under	subclassify, submarine

com-	together, with	committee, cooperate
re-	back, again	return, reject
de-	down	depress, describe
in-	not	incomplete, illegal, irregular
pre-	before	pre-1960, previous
ad-	to, towards	advance, attention

List 2		
Prefix	Meaning	Example word
fore	before	forename, forewarned
post	later, after	post-date, postscript
un	reversal of action	untie; unburden
anti	against	anti-inflation, anti-aircraft
en	forms a verb	encage; enslave, encourage
pro	in favour of	pro-British, pro-abortion
counter	against	counter-attack, counteract
hyper	above, over	hypersensitive, hyperactive
arch	chief	archbishop, archangel
neo	new	neo-colonialism, neoclassical
bi	two	biplane, bicycle, biennial
ab-	away	abstract, abstain
ob-	against	obstruct, oppose
in-	in	instruct, intense

You can introduce prefixes and suffixes in the first years of a learner's schooling, then gradually over the year levels build their knowledge and fluency with prefixes and suffixes. They are especially useful for expanding learners' ability to work out newly encountered words that have prefixes and suffixes. When finding word examples with the prefix or suffix in focus, discussing the word meaning and the specific meaning role or meaning is helpful for learners. Exercises using them can be made fun, incorporating the main optimal conditions for learning. (Appendix 8 has a much larger list of the most useful prefixes and suffixes.)

Justification for the word families and prefixes and suffixes activity

An important way in which young learners expand their vocabulary knowledge is through *morphological problem solving* (seeing relationships between stems and their family members). This activity makes them aware of prefixes and suffixes and gets them familiar with the idea that words have families and are not just separate items. The more frequent a word, the more likely it is to have a lot of family members. Words in the first 1,000 have on average around seven family members. Words in the fifth 1,000 have around four family members, and those in the 16th 1,000 around two. Many of the family members of high-frequency word families are actually infrequent words. You can find 10 lists of 1,000 word families on Paul Nation's website (http://www.victoria.ac.nz/lals/staff/paul-nation.aspx). These lists are not for learners but can be referred to by teachers. This word consciousness focus is ranked high because many English words contain word parts.

4. Word stems

Description

Free stems are usually easy to recognise, but bound stems often require some deliberate attention.

Activity

Here are some questions you can ask to get learners thinking about bound stems:

- Do you think these words are related to each other?
- What related part do they share?
- What does this part mean?
- Do you know any other words with this part with this meaning?

Table 9.5a Pairs of related words for analysis

visit—television	spectacles—specimen
force—effort	superman—supermarket
respect—spectacles	stand—distant
position—deposit	message—missile
reverse—convert	middle—medium

Answers: *vis* = see; *for(t)* = strong; *spec(t)* = see; *pos* = place, put; *vers* = turn around; *super* = above; *sta* = stand; *mess, miss* = send; *mid, med* = middle.

Table 9.5b Pairs of related words for analysis

indicate—dictate	tractor—subtract
form—uniform	generate—gene
attract—tractor	voice—vocabulary
paragraph—graph	decide—scissors
introduce—conductor	second—sequence

Answers: *dic(t)* = say; *form* = shape; *tract* = pull; *graph* = write or draw; *duc* = lead; *tract* = pull; *gen* = produce; *voc* = voice; *cid*, *cis* = cut; *sec*, *sequ* = follow.

(Appendix 7 contains lists of the 125 most useful word stems, with examples. Older learners can be introduced to the etymology section of dictionary entries, and to apps such as Etymology.)

Justification for the word stems activity
Most native speakers are not aware that many words share the same word stem. Becoming aware of this and seeing some of the relationships can make learners very interested in etymology. Often the word stem relationships are between words that came to English through French and Latin. Giving a little of the history of English, particularly the influence of French and Latin on English, can make these relationships even more interesting and understandable. When the stem of a word is known, the word is easier to remember because it can be connected to what is already known.

5. Words in use
Description
Some words work better than other words in certain contexts. Good writers and speakers use words well. Using words well does not just mean using them appropriately, but also using them to good effect.

Activity
When doing shared reading or intensive reading, occasionally point out examples of words being used very well. This clever use may be highlighted by considering what other word could have been used and why this one is better. Here are some examples of clever use.

> **Box 9.1. Questions focusing on word use**
>
> Why is *Slip, slop, slap* a good name for the campaign to prevent sunburn?
> Why is the use of *lazy* in the words of this song a clever use?
>   *A casual stroll through a garden.*
>   *A kiss by a lazy lagoon.*
> What do you think of the use of the phrase *at their feet* in this newspaper headline about soccer players: *Two Argentinians with the world at their feet*? (*Dominion Post*, 6 June 2015).
> Which part of "No" don't you understand?

Justification for the words in use activity

Using language well often requires some thought and planning. When giving a speech, for example, it is important to say things well to get the desired effect. When writing, the words used need to suit the audience and goals of the piece of writing. Being sensitive to the effects of words requires conscious attention.

6. Collocations, figuratives and idioms

Description

Words typically occur in the company of other words, and at times it makes more sense to learn word groups rather than single words. One of the aspects of knowing a word (see Table 3.1) is knowing its collocates. Native speakers pick up collocational knowledge through experience with the language; that is, through listening and reading input. Here are some very frequent collocations: *each other, last night, at the time, on the other hand, make up your mind*. Here are some less frequent but very distinctive collocations: *to and fro, at sixes and sevens, torrential rain, space debris, a diabolical liberty, nose to the grindstone, toe the line*.

Some people call collocations like these idioms, but true idioms are word groups where the meanings of the parts do not make up the meaning of the whole. There are surprisingly only a small number of these in English, around 100. Here are the most common ones: *as well* (meaning *also*), *by and large, of course, take someone to task, red herring*. Most of what people call idioms are really figuratives. Figuratives are collocations that have two meanings—a literal meaning and a figurative meaning. These two meanings are closely related. For example, *gave me the green light* has the literal meaning of being shown a green light. Its figurative meaning is getting permission to do something. It comes from the green (and red) lights used to control traffic and to control car races. Part of the fun in learning figurative expressions is learning where they came from.

About 20% of figuratives make use of some poetic features, most commonly alliteration (words beginning with the same sound); for example: *spick and span, at sixes and sevens, safe and sound*, and *signed and sealed*. Some rhyme, as in *meals on wheels*; *when the cat's away, the mice will play*; or partly rhyme, as in *been and gone, near and far*.

Activity
What are the literal and figurative meanings of these sayings? Where do you think they came from?

Table 9.6a Figurative expressions to discuss

Past your sell-by date	Jumped the gun
Using a carrot and a stick	Rule the roost
A one-man band	A feeding frenzy

Table 9.6b Figurative expressions to discuss

Has her finger on the pulse	Quick off the mark
Go with the flow	On the ropes
Jump in at the deep end	Bite the dust

Here is a web-based source for figurative expressions: http://www.idiomsite.com/.

Justification for the figuratives activity
Figurative expressions are very common, especially in spoken language. We often use them without realising we are doing so. Drawing attention to figuratives is a good introduction to figurative language in general, and to metaphor. Figurative and metaphorical language is often used to influence attitudes to what is being said, and so being aware of it can lead to a more critical understanding of the nature of language use. WordPlosion, explained in Chapter 11, includes a focus on figurative language.

7. Concepts across cultures

Description

The vocabulary of the language reflects what is important to users of that language. It can also shape the way they look at the world. Different languages use different sound systems, different grammar and different vocabulary.

Activity

Table 9.7 Questions focusing on culturally influenced usage

Examining English	Looking at other languages
How many different kinds of bread can you find? Does each have a different name? Do some of these names come to English from other languages?	If you know someone who speaks an Asian language, find out how many words they have for *rice*. Do they have a different word for rice growing in the field, rice for sale in the supermarket, and cooked rice?
What words are used to describe family relationships? For example, mother, father, uncle. Can you draw a chart of these relationships?	Does the same family chart for English work for another language, or do you have to draw a different chart?
What does *dirty* mean? If you blow your nose on a handkerchief and then put it in your pocket, is that dirty? Is it dirty to eat with your hands?	What actions are referred to as dirty in another language that are not dirty in English?
Here are some words in English which came to English from other languages: *sushi, apartment, April, centimetre, chocolate, ski, pizza*. Why were these words borrowed into English?	Here are some words and phrases used in Japanese which have been borrowed from English. *apato* (apartment), salary man, warudo series? Why were these words borrowed into Japanese?

Justification for the concepts across cultures activity

It is good for children to learn that the way the English language works is not the same as the way other languages work. Many learners know other languages and exploring similarities and differences is immensely interesting to them. This encourages them to look more critically at how words are used and can be the beginning of a critical examination of language use and propaganda, where words are used to shape people's attitudes towards other people and events. This field of language study is called 'critical discourse analysis'.

8. Word frequency

Description

A small number of words occur very frequently in a language, while others occur very infrequently. When you learn another language it is a good idea to learn the frequent words first, because you will meet and need them a lot.

Activity

Use the Frequency program at http://www.lextutor.ca to turn one of Aesop's fables into a frequency list. You can get a free electronic copy of Aesop's fables from Project Gutenberg (http://www.gutenberg.org/). Alternatively, if some of your own students' writing is in electronic form, you can analyse their texts using the Frequency program. Look at the frequency list and answer these questions.

- What is the most frequent word? What percentage of the text does it cover? Why is it so frequent?
- Are the frequent words shorter than the less-frequent words?
- Usually around half of the different words occur only once. Is this true in your data?
- Can you draw a graph of the frequency pattern, with frequency on the vertical part of the graph and the different words along the bottom?
- If you do a frequency count on a different story or text, are the frequent words the same or different?
- If you do a frequency count of a text of a similar length from a different language, such as Māori or Samoan, do you get a similar pattern of frequencies?
- Zipf's Law says that the second word in a ranked frequency list will occur with about half the frequency as the most frequent word (the first one in the list), the third word will occur with about one third of the frequency of the most frequent word, the fourth word will occur with one-fourth of the frequency, and so on. Is this true of your frequency list?

Justification for the word frequency activity

The word frequency patterns for all languages are similar, although not exactly the same, and roughly follow Zipf's Law. A few words occur very frequently, and most occur much less frequently. Knowing about the frequency distribution in a language is helpful for teachers to analyse word usage in a text. Learners realise that it is more useful for them to learn the words that are roughly next in the frequency distribution because these will be met and used more often, which means they will get the best return for their learning.

9. Homonyms

Description

Homonyms are words that have the same spelling and pronunciation but very different meanings. The meanings are not connected to each other.

Activity

What are the two meanings of each of these words? How can we know which meaning is being used?

Table 9.8 Homonyms

bowl	band
cricket	bank
patient	fine
club	box
can	light

Answers: *bowl* = deep dish, bowl a ball; *cricket* = game, insect; *patient* = able to wait, sick person; *club* = an organisation, a heavy stick; *can* = able, tin can; *band* = rubber band, music band; *bank* = for money, by a river; *fine* = good, something you pay; *box* = a container, a sport; *light* = not heavy, something that shines.

Other examples are *lie, like, match, mean, miss, pound, pupil, race, right, sock*.

As well as homonyms, there are homographs (words with the same spelling but different pronunciations and meanings, such as row a boat, have a row), and homophones (words with the same pronunciation but different spellings and meanings (bear, bare; their, there).

Table 9.9 Description and examples of homoforms

Name	Examples	Meaning	Spelling	Pronunciation
Homonym	may, May	Different	The same	The same
Homograph	close (shut), close (near)	Different	The same	Different
Homophone	its, it's	Different	Different	The same

Justification for the homonyms activity

About one out of every 10 word families has a homonym for at least one of its family members. Usually the two meanings are very different in their frequency, such that the meaning of one member of the homonym makes up at least 95% of the occurrences of the form. A few homonyms like *bowl* and *miss/Miss* have more equal occurrences. Understanding that some words have homonyms may help learners deal with the occasions when they meet an unknown member of a homonym that does not seem to make sense in context using the meaning they know. Homophones can be a source of spelling problems, with the wrong spelling being used for the similar sounding word which has a different meaning, such as *their* and *there*, or *its* and *it's*.

10. Concordances

Description

A concordance is a list of examples of a word in context. The examples are found by using a computer program (a concordancer) on a collection of texts (a corpus). Here is part of a concordance for the word *dismay*.

Box 9.2 A concordance based on "dismay"

1. … knowledge that their good fortune meant [[dismay]] for their fellow workers in Galway. Man …
2. … was a mistake and we deeply regret the [[dismay]] it has caused to the public and to BBC …
3. … r Scotland. Water rights I read with [[dismay]] the remark attributed to the Central Sc …
4. … ircus is very much in town… much to the [[dismay]] of the greengrocer who provided lunch b …
5. … ingly travellers view the prospect with [[dismay]]. The irony is even though the traveller …
6. … ight the Diocese of Oxford reacted with [[dismay]]. It says wooden crosses as a temporary …
7. … n holiday. The move's been greeted with [[dismay]] by some officials at Gloucester. Nick C …
8. … ble, but the news has been greeted with [[dismay]] by local business leaders. Mark Kiff re …
9. … . She says there's a sense of shock and [[dismay]]. Today Patients and visitors had a simi …
10. … e us this reaction. The court expressed [[dismay]] that Wiltshire Social Services had call …

A concordance can be sorted according to the words on each side of the target word.

Concordances are very useful for finding out how words and phrases are used. Here is a concordance for *in the deep end*.

> **Box 9.3 A concordance based on "in the deep end"**
>
> 1. ... lse. Activists also like being thrown [[in the deep end]] They quite like the challenge of being ...
> 2. ... read and cold milk. That was being put [[in the deep end]] for a start! Well then, also at dusk, ...
> 3. ... rnessed up. It's all new. They put us [[in the deep end]] with everything that came along, you ...
> 4. ... wade towards the awaiting DSP sharks [[in the deep end]]. In practice, a mix of assembly...
> 5. ... he strategically-placed German towels [[in the deep end]]. Oh, and the hire car broke down....
> 6. ... the picture of a man floundering around [[in the deep end]] of life, who has forgotten not only...

Note that only one example, line 5, is not a figurative. A free concordancer, AntConc, is available from http://www.antlab.sci.waseda.ac.jp/software.html. An online concordancer with a corpus is available at http://www.lextutor.ca.

Activity

Learners who are old enough to use concordancers and to interpret concordance data can be given tasks that involve looking up words or phrases to see how they are used. Here are some questions they could try to answer.

> - Is it possible to say "There is three answers" There + is + plural?
> - Which is the most frequent meaning of *bowl*: to bowl a ball, or a container?
> - Do we say *different to*, or *different than*?
> - What is the most common use of *well*?
> - Do people use *whom* much?
> - Is the word *police* usually followed by *is* or *are*?

Justification for the concordances activity

Being able to use a concordancer enables learners to be independent in their study of language use. Concordance data are also more reliable than human intuition, and the use of concordances allows learners to gather data on which to base statements about language and language use. It is thus a very easy and effective introduction to the scientific method, which involves having a theory, gathering data, and then deciding if the data support or do not support the theory. A concordance quickly brings together a lot of contexts that would otherwise be met one by one over a long period of time.

11. Restrictions on the use of words

Description

Some words and word groups have restrictions on their use. For example, they may be largely used in American English, such as *wrench* (the tool), *wait up*, *lucked out*, or British English (*owt*, *scarper*, *blimey*). They may be words used with children (*undies*, *moo-cow*, *pussycat*). They may be very informal words (*kid* = child, *biff* = hit, *ratbag*). Some words are swear words (*damn*, *bloody*). Some words are very uncommon, rare or technical and so are not used in everyday speech and writing (*bifurcate*, *egregious*, *inguinal*). If these words are used in inappropriate situations they may be misunderstood, or seem offensive, strange or unusual.

Activity

Find out the restriction on each of these words or phrases.

Table 9.10 Words with restricted uses

blast!	cookies	yep (yes)
brung (instead of *brought*)	sir (as in "Yes, sir")	momentarily (soon)
hood (the engine cover of a car)	ta (thanks)	see ya (goodbye)
bonnet (the engine cover of a car)	go nigh-nighs (sleep)	chap (a good chap)
plonker	Mum (for *mother*)	expeditiously (quickly, soon)
a biscuit (instead of a scone)	nowt (nothing)	without further ado
notwithstanding	doggie	Pākehā
refurbishment (redecorating)	kids (children)	damn!
drongo	lucked out	It's choice, man
the bog	bro	daddy

The restrictions include: used only in certain countries (for example, in the US but not the UK, or vice versa); an impolite swear word; very informal; used only with children; very low frequency; used on formal occasions; old-fashioned; very infrequent; specialist and technical.

Justification for the restrictions on the use of words activity
Learning about restrictions on words is a good lead-in to the wider idea of using words and language appropriately, both in speaking and in writing.

12. Spelling rules

Description
English seems like a language with very irregular spelling, but in fact there is quite a lot of regularity in the spelling system. Most of the regularity is in the single letter-to- sound correspondences. There are a few more complicated rules that are worth giving some attention to.

Box 9.4 Two spelling rules

Final silent e
Many words in English end in the letter *e*, which is in the spelling but does not seem to be pronounced. This letter is called final silent *e*. Final silent *e* does two main jobs.
1. In words like *same, fine, bone* and *use* it signals that the vowel in front of it has a long (free) sound. The long sounds of single vowels are the names of the letters *a, e, i, o* and *u*, so *a* is pronounced as in *mate*. If final silent *e* was not in the spelling, what would the example words just given sound like: *sam, fin, bon, us*? This effect of final silent *e* is part of a bigger rule, which we will look at next.
2. Final silent *e* signals that the letters in front of it are pronounced in a certain way. Compare the pronunciation of the same consonant letters in these pairs of words: *bag—age, breath—breathe, us—use*. Although these rules are very commonly applied, unfortunately there are also many exceptions.

Free sounds and checked sounds
Each of the vowel letters *a, e, i, o* and *u* has a free pronunciation and a checked (or shortened) pronunciation. The free pronunciation is the same as the names of the vowel letters, so the free pronunciation of *a* is as in *plane*. The checked pronunciation of the vowel letters is as in these words *pan, pen, pin, on, pun*. How do we know from the spelling when to pronounce the letter with the free sound or the checked sound? There is a rule that explains this. The rule applies to stressed syllables. If the vowel is followed by a single consonant letter and another vowel letter, the pronunciation of the vowel will be free. If the stressed vowel is followed by double consonants or the following consonant is the end of the word, then the vowel has a checked (or limited/short) pronunciation.

Free	Checked
late	latter
scene, scenic	pen, penny
dine	dinner, din
hope	hop
super	supper, sup
cure	occurrence

When giving attention to a single spelling–sound correspondence, such as when <u>ou</u> = the vowel sound as in *out* or *house*, there are several points to consider. Learning spelling–sound correspondences occurs in four ways:

- incidentally meeting them in reading, as in shared reading or extensive reading
- using them in writing

- deliberate study
- fluent reading and writing of easy texts.

  Deliberate study can involve:
- seeing a list of words that are known orally, all of which contain the same spelling–sound correspondence, such as *out, house, our, mouth, mountain*
- focusing on a few familiar sight words containing the spelling–sound correspondence
- listening to an explanation of the spelling–sound correspondence, which points out the letter or letters it contains, the sound it represents, and the most frequent words containing it,
- being helped to decode the spelling–sound correspondence in assisted reading or in shared reading
- meeting words containing the spelling–sound correspondence in dictation.

Sounding out words to spell or read is often challenging in English, especially for young learners and new learners of English. This is because their knowledge of sound clusters in English is limited, and so sounding out the word may not result in how the word is spelt or how the word is actually said. Two major factors in the development of English as we use it today have affected this seeming irregularity of pronunciation and spelling: the great vowel shift and the import of foreign words (words from other languages).

To illustrate this, try sounding out the words *thorough* and *crucial* as if you do not know how to spell them. It's challenging. Other words are more aligned, with sound and spelling matching. Assumptions are often made that learners can use the 'sounding out' principle a great deal to work out how to spell a word they know orally. In fact, sounding out words with little knowledge of English sound-letter clusters can often result in misspelling.

The vowel sound in *blue*, for example, can be spelt up to 18 different ways, including *ue, oo, u, ui, o, oe, ou, ough,* and *ew* (*food, truth, fruit, blues, to, shoe, group, through, grew*), but all of these have other pronunciations as well (e.g. as in *flood, trust, build, bluest, go, hoe, grout, rough, sew*). As a rule, it is generally better to help the learner early on to know how the word is spelt and avoid the learner getting frustrated or deciding on a spelling that is far from how it is spelt.

There are some principles that should guide the choice of correspondences and their deliberate teaching.

1. Don't show the same spelling with other pronunciations at the same time: avoid interference.
2. Get the learners to memorise the spelling of the very high frequency words containing the spelling.
3. Help the learners meet plenty of examples.
4. Encourage the learning condition of retrieval when working with the examples. That is, get the learners to study the examples, remove the examples away, then make the learners retrieve them from memory; for example, by dictating the words for the learners to write.

(See http://www.galacticphonics.com/ for a comprehensive list of sound–spelling correspondences.)

Justification for the spelling rules

Spelling is best approached across the four strands: through plenty of reading (meaning-focused input), through writing (meaning-focused output), through deliberate study (language-focused learning) of the rules suggested here and sound–spelling correspondences, and through fluency development, with lots of easy reading and writing. Deliberate study should only be a part—and not too big a part—of spelling improvement. Feedback on writing and memorisation of difficult-to-spell words are other forms of deliberate attention to spelling.

Other word consciousness activities

Several focuses on word consciousness can be brought together in the activity called *word experts* (also called *word detectives* or *word catcher*). In this activity, each learner chooses a word to research. Ideally it is a word that has occurred in their reading or that is important in their study or hobbies. Learners use a variety of sources to gather information on the word's core meaning (found by analysing a dictionary entry or two), spelling (looking for any irregularities in its spelling), origin (using an etymology app or a large dictionary), and some example sentences of its use (from their reading, dictionaries, or an online concordancer or search engine), plus any word parts it contains.

When they are confident in their knowledge of the word, they report on the word to the class, giving their classmates an opportunity to learn the word. When reporting on the word, it is best if the learners work from brief notes so that they have a chance to retrieve what they have deliberately learned. The word expert sheet in Appendix 9 is one way to organise learners' recording as they gather information about the word.

Learning words

As well as knowing about words, learners should also know how to learn and remember words. Because the conditions of noticing, retrieval, varied use and elaboration are important for many kinds of learning besides learning vocabulary, the teacher should show learners how widely these conditions can be applied; for example, using retrieval in the learning of people's names, in remembering what they have just read, and in preparing for exams. The conditions for learning are probably clearest and easiest to remember if they are expressed as a few simple rules.

1. Close your eyes and try to recall what you have just studied or read.
2. Do this at least four or five times for the same material.
3. Space the recall with at least a few minutes between the first recalls and a day or more between later recalls.
4. Use memory tricks such as breaking words into parts, relating stems to known words, learning about the history of a word or phrase, trying to relate the sound of the word to its meaning, visualising the meaning of the word, using the keyword technique, and recalling the context or situation in which the word occurred.
5. After you can recall the meaning of a word when you see it or hear it (receptive recall), try recalling the spoken and written form of the word (productive recall).

When learners are familiar with the meaning and application of these rules, the rules can be shortened to make them easier to remember.

1. Use spaced recall.
2. Do repeated recall.

3. Use memory tricks.
4. Do both receptive recall and productive recall.

If learners memorise these rules, they can act as handy prompts for their learning.

These memory rules are so powerful that spending time over a number of sessions is worthwhile, so that learners understand them and can apply them to a wide variety of learning goals. Learners should eventually be able to look critically at their own learning and decide if they applied the rules well or not. For example, what is good and bad about the following attempts at learning?

> I really worked hard for an hour at learning my history lesson. I read the passage we were supposed to study three times.

> After I read the text I got my classmate to test me on it by asking me questions.

> After reading the text, I closed my book and tried to remember what I had read. The next morning I tried again.

> When I am walking home from school I try to recall the new words I met today.

We can see that consciousness raising about vocabulary covers a wide range of aspects of word knowledge and use. Consciousness raising helps vocabulary learning through deliberate attention to systematic features of the language, and also helps language use through a deeper understanding of words.

Implications for teaching and learning

1. Learners becoming enthusiastic and interested in words is powerful as this in itself enhances the learning conditions needed for learning.
2. Developing word consciousness should be part of a well-thought-out vocabulary programme.
3. There are many focuses for word consciousness, and teachers should decide which ones are most important for their students and focus on them.

4. Each focus of word consciousness involves considerable learning, and it is important to help develop learners' skill in a few focuses rather than cover all of them very quickly and without the learners truly understanding them.

5. Word consciousness focuses involve strategies for gaining information about words, and these strategies should be well practised.

6. It is also useful if learners understand how to learn and are consciously aware of the important learning conditions of repeated encounters, noticing, retrieval, varied use, elaboration and deliberate attention. They should also know how to put these conditions into practice.

Further reading

For an article on word consciousness, see:

J. A. Scott, & W. E. Nagy. (2004). Developing word consciousness. In J. F. Baumann & E. J. Kame'enui (Eds.), *Vocabulary instruction: Research to practice* (pp. 201–217). New York, NY: Guilford Press.

For more on word families and prefixes and suffixes, see:

L. Bauer, & I. S. P. Nation. (1993). Word families. *International Journal of Lexicography*, *6*(4), 253–279.

For an article on the most useful word stems with lots of examples, see:

Z. Wei, & P. Nation. (2013). The word part technique: A very useful vocabulary teaching technique. *Modern English Teacher*, *22*(1), 12–16.

For an article on collocations with plenty of examples, see:

R. Martinez, & N. Schmitt. (2012). A phrasal expressions list. *Applied Linguistics*, *33*(3), 299–320.

For a description of Zipf's law, see:

C. J. Sorell. (2012). Zipf's law and vocabulary. In C. A. Chapelle (Ed.), *Encyclopaedia of applied linguistics*. Oxford, UK: Wiley-Blackwell. http://onlinelibrary.wiley.com/doi/10.1002/9781405198431.wbeal1302/abstract

For an article on figuratives with plenty of examples, see:

F. Boers, J. Eyckmans, & H. Stengers. (2007). Presenting figurative idioms with a touch of etymology: More than mere mnemonics? *Language Teaching Research*, *11*(1), 43–62.

For a list of the sound–spelling correspondences of English, see the appendix of:

I. S. P. Nation. (2009). *Teaching ESL/EFL reading and writing.* New York, NY: Routledge.

Resources

The Frequency program at http://www.lextutor.ca.

Chapter 10 Helping learners with below-average vocabulary sizes

Young learners who from birth have experienced plentiful directed and undirected talk, and who have been read to often, accompanied by talk, both in their early years and throughout their early school years, will gain vocabulary and knowledge, and will be advantaged in their comprehension of what they hear and read, and in expressing their thinking, ideas and knowledge. A child reading or read to for close to an hour a day will increase their vocabulary merely because they are encountering large numbers of words. A child involved in elaborated talk, who often participates in quality conversations and listens to high-quality and engaging audio and other forms of spoken texts—more than simple routine exchanges—will also encounter large numbers of words, some of which will be in their Goldilocks zone.

Learners who have smaller than average vocabulary sizes are likely to be struggling to express themselves confidently and fully in speaking, will struggle with reading, and as a result will be slow in increasing their vocabulary size. Some learners may well have considerable gaps in understanding the language and in being able to express their ideas strongly because they are relatively new learners of the language, or because their families mostly use languages other than the target language with them. Such learners will benefit from a great deal of talk and reading, accompanied by many opportunities to try out their growing capabilities in their new or less-used language. It is important to stress here that strengths in languages other than English are treasures. Knowing more than one language is always a plus.

The most important way to help learners with a small vocabulary size, no matter the language, is to provide them with an abundance of engaging, comprehensible language. Two prime sources are spoken language in which they participate in some way, and reading. Plenty of reading at the right level, accompanied by talk and interaction with others, will expand learners' word knowledge. Reading for such learners is best accompanied by some deliberate attention to vocabulary. This can involve vocabulary learning through talk, before and during reading about the words arising during reading.

The first step, however, is to look carefully at the struggling learner to see where their problem lies, and to see if vocabulary knowledge is a problem or not.

Diagnosing vocabulary and reading problems

If you feel that a large number of learners in the class have problems, then initially it may be best to choose just two or three typical learners to look at closely and work with individually, so that you can get an accurate idea of the scope and nature of the difficulties each learner faces.

Appendix 2 describes the freely available Picture Vocabulary Size Test. This can be used for testing young learners who cannot read or who struggle with reading. Reading well must first and foremost be reading to understand. Knowing words, being able to read words fluently, and knowing word meanings combine so that a learner can read fluently and confidently with a strong focus on meaning.

As we saw in Chapter 3, we would expect 5-year-olds to have a vocabulary size of at least 3,000 word families, and 8-year-olds should know around 5,000 word families. The Picture Vocabulary Size Test tests words up to the sixth 1,000 word level. The test is computer-based and a learner can sit the test in about 15 to 20 minutes. The test can be downloaded from Laurence Anthony's website: http://www.laurenceanthony.net/software/pvst/. There is a set of instructions and specifications accompanying the test in the Help menu.

Guidelines for helping learners with below-average vocabulary sizes

In the following guidelines the first seven apply to the whole class, regardless of whether they are doing well in their literacy and regardless of their vocabulary size. The remaining guideline is directed mainly towards learners with below-average vocabulary sizes.

1. Create a culture of conversation throughout all teaching and learning activities and tasks—with a partner, in small and large groups, and in guided and unguided tasks. Talking conversationally with learners, with the teacher participating and using words and language structures that are in the Goldilocks zone of the learners, provides important opportunities for vocabulary growth. With deliberate 'gifting' of 'cutting-edge' vocabulary, learners can potentially learn and use vocabulary they otherwise might not. Engaging in cutting-edge talk is not only good for general learning, but also a key contributor to learners' vocabulary growth.

2. Create a rich menu of spoken texts that are meaningful and comprehensible to the learners. There is a wide variety of retrievable spoken text sources and resources learners can engage with, both guided and unguided. As discussed in Chapter 6, audio-only and audio-accompanied visual/print texts have the potential to increase learners' vocabulary knowledge. By providing learners with such texts in class, or by suggesting listening to them out of class time, teachers can be sure learners will learn new words and reinforce partially known words.

3. Find reading material that is suited to the learners' level and interests, and make sure plenty of reading is done.

4. With the learner—and their family, when appropriate—set specific reading goals to read close to an hour a day. This reading can include reading for a variety of purposes and need not be reading at one sitting. The critical factor is that reading mileage matters, and setting reading as part of daily routines is a way of ensuring reading happens. It doesn't matter very much if some of the reading seems a little easy. The nature of language is such that even easy reading will contain some words that are likely to be only partly known to a young reader.

5. With the whole class, develop word consciousness. Word consciousness involves having a positive attitude towards and interest in words so that noticing words occurs. It is about knowing a range of things about words, such as:

- some words occur very often and many words are very infrequent
- words occur with other words in common sayings and word groups
- carefully choosing the words you use can make communication much more effective
- some words contain prefixes, suffixes and stems
- different uses of the same word share a core meaning
- some words have the same form but unrelated meanings
- some words can only be used in certain situations
- dictionaries provide a lot of useful and interesting information about words
- most words follow spelling rules.

Word consciousness was looked at in detail, with plenty of examples and activities, in Chapter 9. The goals of word consciousness are to make learners aware of the usefulness of giving attention to words and aware of how to give words attention so they are learned. It also engenders a lifelong love of and interest in words.

6. With the whole class, give quick attention to vocabulary in a systematic way. In Chapter 8 we looked at ways of quickly giving attention to words by focusing on their meaning, form and use—sometimes called quick glossing. Teachers need to become aware of what they can focus on and how to do this quickly. This kind of quick attention does not require any preparation by the teacher, but does require the teacher to be aware of what words are best focused on (generally mid-frequency, Goldilocks-zone, topic-related words), and how to focus on them. Studies have shown that by quickly giving attention to words, vocabulary learning can be increased. When the vocabulary that is focused on also occurs in reading texts, then the chances of meeting words again and learning them are much greater. When the vocabulary that is focused on is oral, then enhanced noticing as part of the quick attention will be needed.

7. Engage the learners in discussions to build understanding and provide opportunities to use topic-related vocabulary. Language use enriches and strengthens vocabulary knowledge. To expand their

vocabulary, learners need to move beyond the vocabulary they already know well and engage with vocabulary at the edge of their knowledge—what some have called 'frontier' or 'cutting-edge' vocabulary. Vocabulary knowledge reflects life experience. In other words, the more learners experience new things accompanied by talk and text, the richer their vocabulary knowledge is likely to be. In school this experience should occur through the school subjects. Vocabulary learning is helped by re-encountering the same words and through quality of processing. Teachers should build these conditions into subject-focused activities by coming back to the same topic in different ways so that learners meet the topic-related vocabulary both receptively and productively, and in varied contexts. This can be done through focused discussion, reporting back on the discussion, seeking relevant ideas through reflection and reading, and writing about what was discussed.

8. For learners with below-average vocabulary sizes, work with individuals or groups of learners using intensive, focused reading approaches. The following section looks at this kind of reading.

Intensive reading

Intensive reading involves the teacher working on a text with learners, focusing on deepened understanding of what the text is about and exploring vocabulary related to the story or text. A major aim of intensive reading is to understand the various levels of text meaning. Another is to increase learners' language knowledge and reading skills. Intensive reading is seen as being part of language-focused learning because it has this language learning and skills development aim and involves deliberate attention to language features that provide text meaning.

When learners take part in shared reading, the first session with a particular book might be a kind of intensive reading. The later sessions on the same book become more like independent reading and listening as meaning-focused input and fluency development.

In addition to shared reading as a class activity, it is beneficial for learners with below-average vocabulary to share read in smaller, more homogeneous groups while other learners get on with independent reading. This allows the teacher to focus more intensively on the learners' unknown and partially known vocabulary. However, it is also important to remember that frequent grouping of similarly capable learners does not provide the benefit of more capable learners being a source of 'cutting edge' vocabulary and expression for the less capable learners. Multi-level grouping can do this. With the teacher there to scaffold the more capable learners, and guide the availability of cutting edge expression from them to less capable learners, every learner has the potential to gain.

An individual learner reading aloud to the teacher is also a form of intensive reading. The teacher provides support during the reading, supporting fluency development and, most importantly, guiding the learner to a deeper understanding of what they are reading. The *pause, prompt, praise* procedure is often suggested as being helpful during such sessions. In an ideal situation, parents engage in such reading with their child at home too. Appendix 4 contains a description of a procedure that could be used to guide parents to help with their child's reading and vocabulary development.

The focuses and practice of intensive reading are outlined in Table 10.1.

A balanced vocabulary development programme

Meaning-focused input

In a balanced vocabulary development programme about a quarter of the time is spent on incidental vocabulary learning through reading and engaging with spoken texts. All this requires from the teacher in terms of vocabulary development is that the learners have plenty of independent reading opportunities at the right level for each learner, and there are opportunities to meet new vocabulary in challenging and supportive spoken-language contexts.

Meaning-focused output

About a quarter of the time is spent on talking and writing that is appropriate to the learners' reading and spoken language experience. Talking and writing should encourage them to use the vocabulary they know and have met in reading and oral work. This productive use of vocabulary can be encouraged by very closely relating the talking topic and writing to what they read and experience. Linked learning and theme-based focuses and tasks are excellent for doing this.

Table 10.1. Focuses and techniques in intensive reading

Language and skill focus	Techniques
Visuals	• Reading materials for young learners usually include visuals—photos or drawings. These act to interest the learner and draw them into the text. They usually link to meanings and vocabulary in the print text. • Talking about the visuals and making links with the print support learners' fluency and comprehension. **Note:** Using visuals to guess the word in print is a strategy many young or new learners of reading use to get at the printed words. They will need to be scaffolded to focus on the written word and read it, if this word is to become one they can read fluently.
Punctuation	• Draw attention to question marks, exclamation marks and quotation marks, and their purpose. • When reading out loud, support the learners to read observing text punctuation, and to reading flowingly, using varying voice modulations.
Vocabulary	• Quickly give the meanings of difficult or unknown words. • There is potential vocabulary 'within' the visuals. There is vocabulary in the print. Explore the meanings of words with learners, especially new or partially known words. • Also draw attention to the spelling or pronunciation of words.
Grammar	• Words cluster in meaningful groups. Discuss groups of words: they often carry extended meanings compared to single words.
Word recognition	• Read along with learners to support their fluent reading of words and text. As the learner gains confidence and fluency, carefully withdraw the support.
Comprehension skills	• Encourage prediction and retelling. • Help the learners relate the text to personal experience, and to what they know and think. This helps learners to meaningfully connect to the text they are reading. • Discuss characters in the story, moments of surprise and tension—in fact, anything the learner or you find interesting.

Language-focused learning

About a quarter of the time should be spent deliberately focusing on vocabulary and word consciousness activities. Over a school week this might take up to no more than an hour or two. In addition, the learners could have about an hour or two of intensive reading per week.

Fluency development

About a quarter of the time should be spent working with very easily comprehended texts and easy material across the four language skills of listening, speaking, reading, and writing. This might involve both planned and spontaneous discussions and conversations, re-reading books, reading print that is easy at an independent or close to independent level for the learner, re-meeting what has been read or talked about across several shared reading sessions, and linking meaningful tasks to materials already encountered. Table 10.2 summarises this information about the four strands.

Table 10.2. A balanced vocabulary programme for young native speakers

Strand	Percentage of time	Activities
Meaning-focused input	25%	Independent reading Audio tasks and opportunities Linked skills activities
Meaning-focused output	25%	Speaking/discussions Message-focused writing Linked skills activities
Language-focused learning	25%	Learning about vocabulary Word consciousness raising Intensive reading
Fluency development	25%	Reading easily comprehended materials Re-reading and revisiting previously supported materials, topics and texts Linked skills activities and tasks

Implications for teaching and learning

1. Foreground with families the key role that talk and 'gifting' spoken language can play in expanding their child's vocabulary.

2. Ensure there are many opportunities for learners to engage in meaningful oral language exchanges and listening during a school day.

3. Develop clear reading goals with each learner and their family, and for teaching, so that there is a balance of the strands (as in Table 10.2).

4. Support learners with below-average vocabulary sizes with large quantities of 'gifting' talk and reading, daily shared reading, independent reading, and audio-supported reading. The material needs to be at the right level for each learner.

5. Diagnose each learner's capabilities carefully on a one-to-one basis, checking their vocabulary size, their reading skills and their oral language strengths and gaps.
6. Create a culture of word consciousness so that each learner is keen and motivated to improve their learning of vocabulary and their use of words. There is a wide range of interesting ways to do this.
7. Make intensive reading with the whole class, small groups and individual learners a regular undertaking in the class. This should include a strong focus on vocabulary and reading skill development.
8. With the learners and their families, and through planned programming, ensure learners have a good balance of vocabulary learning opportunities across the four strands.

Further reading

The classic second-language study on increasing language learning through large quantities of reading is:

W. B. Elley, & F. Mangubhai. (1981). *The impact of a book flood in Fiji primary schools*. Wellington: New Zealand Council for Educational Research.

This short, very readable report is highly recommended reading for teachers of English as a second or foreign language, and also has useful messages for teachers of native speakers. It essentially shows that greatly increasing the quantity of independent reading results in a wide range of language learning benefits. This increase in reading was not an increase in time spent learning English but occurred during normal class time. Reading replaced most teacher-led activities.

Chapter 11 Vocabulary learning procedures

This chapter looks at how the suggestions in the previous chapters of the book can be brought together in more complex activities and sequences of work. Most of the activities involve *rich instruction*, whereby the teacher spends a considerable amount of time on a word looking at several aspects of what is involved in knowing a word. These can range across the form, meaning and use of the word. All approaches described here have been developed by van Hees and have been fully trialed. Done well, each and together have the potential to significantly impact on learners' vocabulary knowledge growth, alongside developing their thinking and interactional capabilities.

WordPlosion

WordPlosion is a vocabulary activity that creates layers of increasing depth of meaning and association using one word as the starting point. The starting-point word might be a focus topic word or a word of particular interest to the learners. For example, learners at school might be studying *Peace and War*, or *Dinosaurs*. The WordPlosion starting point word might be *peace* or *war* or *dinosaur*. Choosing a 'just right' word is a bit subjective, but some words are better than others. It may be better, for example, to choose the word *prehistoric* as the starting point rather than *dinosaur*, in order to first create a wider contextual base before a closer focus on dinosaurs.

WordPlosion can be used with a small or large group of learners. The more learners in the group, the greater the potential to expand their vocabulary scope and meaning-making. However, a larger group requires closer attention to inclusive participation and sharing.

Pair or partner talk followed by collaborative group sharing is central to WordPlosion, as is justifying and explaining. Throughout all the stages and steps, ensure the students are fully participatory: offering their thinking, expressing their ideas fully, and being scaffolded to expand their word knowledge conceptually and linguistically.

WordPlosion has three main parts:

- Part 1: *Focusing on the word's core underlying meaning and use*
- Part 2: *Focusing on the word's family*
- Part 3: *Bringing in words associated with the focus word.*

There is an option of including two further parts:

- Part 4: *Arranging words on a distance continuum from the focus word*
- Part 5: *Identifying and explaining related topic word sayings and expressions.*

A brief outline of each part follows. For the purposes of this outline, the word *prehistoric* is the focus word. Recording along the way by taking notes is recommended, either with the learners recording as WordPlosion proceeds or with the teacher recording. The teacher taking notes is often preferable to ensure the process remains fluid and dynamic, and doesn't become a spelling and writing exercise.

Part 1: Exploring the focus word's core underlying meaning and use

Easy layer: Get the learners to check that they can fluently say, read and write the word.

Core underlying meaning: Explain the word's meaning clearly and precisely using age- and stage-appropriate expression.

RULE: The word cannot be used to explain the word's meaning.

Contextual word use: Shaping up fluent, well-structured sentences using the word appropriately.

EXAMPLE: *prehistoric*
Easy level: Say-ready ✓, read-ready ✓, write-ready ✓
Core meaning: *Of a time before (pre) any recorded history; long, ago, before civilised humans*
Contextual use: *In prehistoric times, some animals were unimaginably huge and different to animals alive today.*
The world was a different place in prehistoric times with no civilisation as we know it now.
Prehistoric animals roamed the earth millions of years ago and we can still find fossils today.

Part 2: The focus word's family

Members of the focus word's family are identified and explained. In pairs first, then as a group, have learners identify and explain members of the word's family, discuss them grammatically (where relevant), and use them contextually. Some words have a small number of word family members while others have many. *Prehistoric* has a small word family:

prehistoric: prehistorical, prehistory, historic, history, historical

Part 3: Words associated with the focus word

This part opens up a wide range of possible associates. Be open to consider all contributions. Suggested associating words may include word groups as well as single-item vocabulary.

RULE: When suggestions are made by learners, they need to explain how their suggestions associate with the focus word.

Examples for *prehistoric:*

roaming—prehistoric animals were largely roaming animals, perhaps walking large distances

climate change—at the time of prehistoric animals the climate was probably quite different to our climate now; maybe a sudden change in climate caused dinosaurs to struggle to survive

a major catastrophe—some scientists think there was a major catastrophe on earth that caused prehistoric animals and plants to die out or vanish

fascinating—to us now it is fascinating to imagine what prehistoric times were like.

Ideally, as many learners as possible nominate an association and offer a reason why it associates. Justification or explanation can usually not be wrong if it is an association that makes sense to the learner. It is then a valid contribution and should be accepted. Scaffolding the contributor to express more fully is part of the value of this part of WordPlosion.

When using WordPlosion with younger learners or for the first time, or with learners who struggle to nominate ideas that associate with the focus word, it is best that associations nominated by the teacher be put up for learners to consider and explain why these associate with the focus word. In this way, available ideas are considered meaningful without the struggle of learners trying to come up with their own initially. This serves to have available 'Goldilocks zone' expression that is deeply processed by the learners through participatory talk and as a model of eventually learners suggesting their own.

At this point, quite some depth about the focus word—including its associated concepts and vocabulary—has been explored through talk and recording. Proceeding on to Parts 4 and 5 is optional. These parts deepen meaning-making about the focus word even more, but could well be omitted.

Part 4: Arranging words on a distance continuum from the focus word

The idea in this part is to push the learners' thinking about the word conceptually, as well as to push their expression. Careful explanation is needed for learners to understand what this part involves. It is best done by giving examples.

Create a continuum line based on the focus word. First you, then the learners in pairs and sharing as a group, suggest words or word groups related to the focus word because they convey a 'nearby' or 'further/far away' concept in relation to the focus word. As with Part 3, there is seldom a wrong contribution. As long as the learner can justify or explain the association and its distance to the focus word, it is a valid contribution and should be accepted.

Note: The idea is not simply to identify similarities and opposites but to offer an opportunity to explore more richly and widely. It may be that only a limited number of words are considered, but even a few are well worthwhile in terms of vocabulary growth, as well as conceptual growth and expanding learners' language knowledge.

Examples for *prehistoric*:

the Middle Ages—far from: *the Middle Ages were only hundreds of years ago while prehistoric is millions of years ago*

creation—quite far from: *the creation of the earth and universe occurred probably millions and millions of years before the time we call prehistoric*

climate change—both far from and close to: *probably before, during and after what is called prehistoric times, climate change was occurring.*

Note: Exploring synonyms and antonyms may be worthwhile here and can be approached in a similar way to the above. It might be preferable to use the word 'like' or 'unlike' the focus word rather than 'synonyms' and 'antonyms'. Semantically, synonyms or antonyms are not the 'same as' or 'different from', but somewhat like or unlike the word in focus.

Part 5: Identifying and explaining related topic word sayings and expressions

There are probably no sayings and expression that directly use the focus example word, *prehistoric*. However, there are sayings and expressions that encapsulate an aspect of the core underlying meaning associated with the word *prehistoric*. We suggest explaining and discussing only a handful of associated sayings and expressions. Many learners have a limited repertoire of these metaphorical forms of making meaning in a language. A good site to refer to for a beginning range of idioms and expressions in English is:

http://www.learn-english-today.com/idioms/idioms_proverbs.html

Usually, learners cannot nominate examples, and so the teacher needs to provide them for consideration and discussion. Possible examples for *prehistoric* are:

change the face of: *whatever happened in prehistoric times, changes since then have 'changed the face' of life on earth as we know it now*

dead as a dodo: *most, if not all, prehistoric plants and animals are 'dead as a dodo'—that is, they are extinct*

race against time: *for many prehistoric life forms, their extinction was a 'race against time' and the inevitable changes occurring on earth and in the universe.*

WordPlosion is an extended word expansion procedure, one that executed over the course of a week provides rich, wide and deep word knowledge. It is expressively valuable and dynamic if done well. Throughout all the above you may provide more or less scaffolding. If the learners have limited ideas and suggestions, the teacher simply offers them, thereby expanding their repertoire and potential acquisition.

Sharing vocabulary through group brainstorming

This activity expands individuals' topic-related vocabulary knowledge by collectively gifting and receiving words, and deepens the comprehension of shared vocabulary by explaining associations. The activity takes about 20 to 30 minutes (van Hees, 2014).

1. *Introduce the topic*

   The students in pairs share current knowledge and thinking about the topic. Then, as a class, they look at topic-related visuals one at a time. The students can be encouraged to make spontaneous responses about the visuals and their thoughts on them.

2. *Brainstorming round 1*

   Using a recording sheet, individual students write down any words or word groups that come to mind while viewing the visuals (about 5–10 minutes). At the same time, you record the words and word groups on paper or card strips, also writing down topic-related vocabulary items the students may not think of or know. Also write down some the students are likely to write down.

   The students, in pairs, then share their list of words and word groups orally with each other. Turn-by-turn, each student calls out one word or word group on their sheet. Their partner checks if they also wrote down this word or word group. If so, they tick it; if not, they add it to their list. As each student nominates a word or word group, they explain why in their thinking it is related to the topic.

Their partner may add to this explanation or challenge its relatedness. By consensus they either retain or delete the item.

Together students check for spelling accuracy, and continue until all words and word groups are shared. Throughout this, the teacher roves around to monitor the process and gauge vocabulary range.

3. *Brainstorming round 2*

    As a class group the students take turns to share one word or word group from their list. As in Round 1, the student who nominates explains why in their thinking it is related to the topic. You and other students may add to this explanation or challenge its relatedness. Class consensus decides whether to retain or throw the item away.

    Each nominated item is checked by the other students. If they also have it, they underline it. If not, they add it to their list. They check for spelling accuracy.

4. *Brainstorming round 3*

    As a class group, the teacher shares her vocabulary items by showing one card strip at a time. As with Rounds 1 and 2, the students check their list. If the item is there, they circle it. If not, they add it. Following each show and check, the students in pairs try to explain or challenge item relatedness. Before moving to the next item, this is shared as in round 2. They check for spelling accuracy.

5. *Group stocktake*

    As a class group the students share ideas about the topic they gained throughout the brainstorming process. The students almost certainly have more ideas about and understanding of the topic and are better able to express this.

This brainstorming approach can be used at the beginning of a topic to establish key ideas, or along the way, or at the end as a stocktake and review.

A valuable next step is to move onto a semantic-mapping task (see Appendix 6). Students in pairs or small groups sort and group the vocabulary on the final list: cutting up their list, discussing possible ways of grouping and why, and creating headings under which to sort the vocabulary. Grouping and placement should be based on consensus, with each item thoroughly discussed. It should not simply become a sort-and-place exercise with minimal dialogue and meaning sharing. This word mapping can lead on to writing.

Word-focused rich instruction using high-frequency vocabulary

Many high-frequency words are simple to understand and use in their most concrete sense. However, for learners unfamiliar with metaphorical and 'cultural' uses of a word, the less concrete uses of the word may be incomprehensible or puzzling, or even totally unfamiliar. It is valuable to explore the nuances of known vocabulary on a regular basis, or at relevant moments with the learners.

An example follows, using *hand* as the example word. The example is pitched to learners of English who have a reasonably strong grasp of basic English already.

Step 1: Introducing the selected vocabulary item

The selected vocabulary item may be directly related to a topic in hand or one that learners identify that arises in class or that you consider worthy of attention.

- Identify and share the word with the learners, including its oral and written form.
- With a visual or the real thing available, develop a concise and precise explanation of the word, first with the students thinking on their own, followed by pair and group sharing.
- If some learners know another language, they can share the spoken and written form of *hand* in that language.
- Use the learners' contribution to develop a fuller explanation: *the end part of a person's arm from the wrist, made up of the palm, four fingers and one thumb; the grasping part at the end of a person's arm used for picking up and holding things.*
- Use a range of dictionaries to look up the word and compare the definitions.
- Develop fluency in expressing the word, giving the definition and using the word in contextually relevant sentences.
- Learners might take notes on parts of the above.

Step 2: Identifying its word family

- On their own and then in pairs, have the learners identify words in the word family, saying and writing down each word family member. If the learners cannot nominate many word family members, offer them some.
- Share the list of word family members as a class by taking turns to nominate one. Each nomination should include:
    - writing up the word for all to see
    - pronouncing the word
    - explaining the word
    - using the word in relevant contextual sentences

    e.g. hands, handy, handed, handle, handful, unhand (me).
- Discuss the family members, each time discussing the link to the underlying meaning. This provides a good opportunity for repetition and strengthening of what has been covered about the word so far.

Step 3: Looking at phrases and expressions using the word

- Have the learners identify, in pairs, phrases or expressions they may know, have heard or have read using the word.
- As in Step 2, have them share what they know as a group, with the teacher contributing, and compile a list. Often the learners may have few word groups or expressions to offer because they are unfamiliar with more metaphorical and cultural uses of the word. The teacher's 'on hand' list might be a main source for inclusion.
- With a list of about 10 word groups and expressions, discuss the meaning, especially identifying how the underlying meaning of the word informs the meaning of the phrase or expression. Here are some examples.

    lay a hand on something, hand in glove, go hand in hand, hand over fist, have a hand in something, be in someone else's hand, to hand over, out of hand, turn your hand to something, a hand to mouth existence, to be handed something on a plate, to keep your hands off, to have time on your hands, a bird in the hand is worth two in the bush

- Explain to the learners that some senses are closely related to the underlying meaning while others seem not to be: more or less congruent; more or less literal; more or less metaphorical. Explain and discuss the meaning of 'literal', 'congruent' and 'metaphorical'.
- Create a continuum:

    Most LITERAL   Least LITERAL   Most METAPHORICAL
- One at a time, each phrase or expression is explored for meaning and use. Simple drawings or a role play may assist explanation and development of understanding.
- Have the learners decide where each phrase and expression might be placed along the continuum, discussing in pairs ready to share with the group. When sharing they should be ready to justify their decision to the group.
- As a group, fully discuss the meaning, usage and placement of each expression on the various continua.

Step 4: Phrase-expression scenario and anecdote matching

- Develop little scenarios or anecdotes linked to or using a phrase or expression. Depending on the capability of the learners, after an example shaped up together these might be composed in pairs to share, or composed as a group, or teacher-provided. Teacher-provided examples offer the learners mileage with reading and meaning-making without struggling with composition.
- In provided examples, the learners in pairs and as a group may (a) read the text, (b) identify the phrases or expressions in the text using the focus word, and (c) discuss why they make sense and are appropriate in the anecdote.

    Example 1: He was nearly 80 years old and quite fit for his age. In former years he'd been a leading-edge scientist—a biologist, in fact. After retirement he said to his family, 'I'm starting my own fish farm. I've got time on my hands now and I want to keep my hand in the area of biology I love best—fish hatching and fish preservation'.

    Example 2: She was always nervous when she stepped onto a plane. While she knew her safety and getting to the destination was in the hands of a fully trained, experienced pilot, she found it hard to relax.

There was, of course, no other choice. Flying as a passenger went hand in hand with letting go and placing her trust in the flying crew. (see Coxhead, 2014).

A final word

Each teacher will have vocabulary learning activities and approaches they favour. These should be looked at critically to see how well they set up the conditions of recycling, noticing, retrieval, varied use, elaboration and deliberate attention that help vocabulary learning to occur. Analysing teaching and learning approaches is an important teacher skill that needs to be accompanied by the skill of adapting an activity to include some of those conditions.

Vocabulary size is a major factor affecting the academic achievement of young children. It is also a symptom, probably due to a lack of experience with a range of large and small topic areas that would provide the opportunity to meet and learn words in meaningful contexts. The approaches suggested in this book involve increasing this experience through wide and substantial reading and listening in a range of topic areas, through challenging and engaging spoken interaction, and through a deliberate focus on vocabulary at the general level of strategies and word consciousness, and at the particular level of word learning.

Appendices

Appendix 1 High-frequency, mid-frequency and low-frequency words

The goal of this activity is to see if you can recognise the three frequency levels of vocabulary. You can practise for this activity by looking at the words in the test in Appendix 3.

The activity

The following list contains 10 high-frequency words, 20 mid-frequency words and 10 low-frequency words. Classify the 40 words into those three groups.

perestroika	recuperate	onomatopoeia	interesting
hierarchy	afraid	expect	ulema
accept	phobia	urethane	obdurate
Baptist	edge	if	lacquer
upbraid	reindeer	nicotine	neurotic
add	operant	lax	converge
orca	enjoy	juvenile	important
perjury	congested	imagine	unctuous
botany	flicker	flourish	osteoarthritis
hatch	bribe	umbrage	laborious

The answers

High frequency	Mid-frequency	Low frequency
accept	**4th & 5th 1,000s**	obdurate
add	Baptist	onomatopoeia
afraid	botany	operant
edge	bribe	orca
enjoy	congested	osteoarthritis
expect	converge	ulema
if	flicker	umbrage
imagine	flourish	unctuous
important	hatch	upbraid
interesting	hierarchy	urethane
	juvenile	
	8th & 9th 1,000s	
	laborious	
	lacquer	
	lax	
	neurotic	
	nicotine	
	perestroika	
	perjury	
	phobia	
	recuperate	
	reindeer	

Appendix 2 *The Picture Vocabulary Size Test*

Overview

The Picture Vocabulary Size Test (Anthony & Nation, 2017) is a test of receptive listening vocabulary size. The test measures whether the test-taker can find a suitable meaning for a specific, partly contextualised word form. It is a recognition test primarily intended for young pre-literate native speakers up to 8 years old, and for non-native speakers. There are two versions of the test using different items but following the same design procedures. The test was designed by Paul Nation, programmed by Laurence Anthony, and trialled by Nation and van Hees in a number of New Zealand primary schools. The test can be downloaded from Laurence Anthony's website http://www.laurenceanthony.net/software/pvst/.

The test is based on the most frequent 6,000 word families of English for young children. There is likely to be a ceiling effect on the test if it is used with native speakers of English who are more than 8 years old; that is, older learners will be likely to have a larger vocabulary size than that shown by the test. A fuller description of the test comes with the test program in the Help tab.

The format is four-item multiple-choice, which can be set up to include an *I don't know* option (illustrated by '?'), as an answer needs to be provided for every item.

Figure A2.1 A screenshot of part of the Picture Vocabulary Size Test

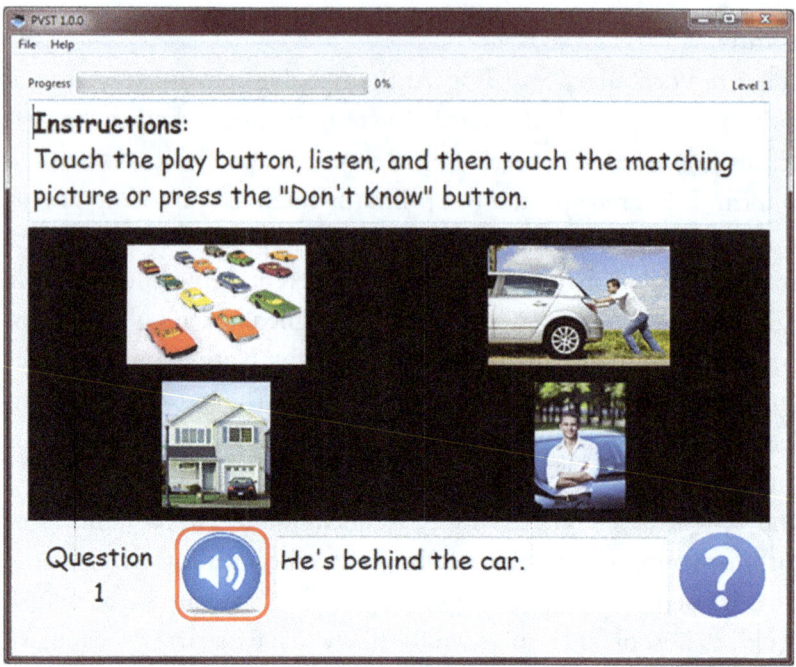

The test is delivered on a computer (tablet or laptop) with a touch screen. The learner hears the test word and the sentence containing each test word and has to touch the most appropriate picture. There is no time limit on the test. It takes around 15 to 20 minutes to sit the whole test.

Because the Picture Vocabulary Size Test is primarily intended for use with younger primary school children from the ages of 5 or 6 up to 7 or 8 years, its administration needs to take account of the fact that the younger children are experiencing cognitive, social, emotional, and physical growth, and are learning literacy skills. It is important that test taking is not daunting and the learner understands the process and feels comfortable with making choices from a selection (McKay, 2006). In essence, this means that the test needs to be administered one-on-one in a strongly supportive and flexible way to take account of the individual test taker. The design of the test—with its use of colourful pictures, oral and written cues, matching format, and tablet-based delivery involving pointing and touching—also takes account of the young age of its users.

The safest interpretation of the results of the test is to look for positive results. That is, to use the test with the goal of excluding vocabulary size as a factor negatively affecting performance (e.g. a learner's reading comprehension). This kind of interpretation assumes there are minimum vocabulary sizes that are sufficient for the performance of certain tasks at various age levels. For example, a child with a receptive listening vocabulary size of 4,000 word families knows enough vocabulary to learn to read English without vocabulary size being a major issue negatively affecting this learning. They may have a sight vocabulary problem, but that is different from listening vocabulary size. On the other hand, a learner aged 8 or 9 years with a similar vocabulary size is likely struggle with the more complex texts likely to be used during teaching and learning in his or her classroom.

As part of this positive approach to interpreting the results of this test, it is important to regard poor results on the Picture Vocabulary Size Test as a reason for doing further investigation of a particular learner's vocabulary size. This investigation would need to look for possible reasons for poor performance on the test. This would include looking at:

- the administration of the test to see if that was a cause of poor performance
- bias in the test through the pictures used or the computerised presentation
- the child's vision and hearing
- the child's feelings about being tested
- the child's understanding of the test process and coping strategies
- whether English is the child's first language or is clearly an additional language
- how long the child has been learning English if it is not their first language.

It is very important that poor performance on the test is carefully investigated to make sure the result truly represents the child's knowledge. At the very least, poor performance on the test should be checked by administering the other version of the test at a different time under the most favourable supportive circumstances.

Interpreting test results

Each test word represents 62.5 words in the source lists. So, a learner's score on the test needs to be multiplied by 62.5 to get their total vocabulary size. Thus, a learner with a score of 54 has a receptive vocabulary size of 3,375 word families.

There can be wide variation of vocabulary size at any particular age level. (See Table 1.1 in Chapter 1 for guidelines.)

Because the test is a sensitive receptive recognition test, it gives credit for partial knowledge. This means that getting a word right on the test does not necessarily mean the word is well known.

Increasing validity through test administration

One-on-one administration of the test ensures each learner remains engaged and does not employ random guessing. When administering the test, it is useful to ensure that all learners are aware of the following.

1. They should look at all four pictures when considering choices.
2. They can touch the number again to hear a sentence again.
3. They can change their mind about a choice by touching a different picture.

Each of the three procedures should be pointed out to each learner with a demonstration, and you should be watching each learner to ensure they perform each procedure where needed. Some learners seem to vary the order of pushing the numbers just for the sake of variety. Where learners respond too quickly, ask them if they looked at all four pictures, encourage them to do that, and praise them for doing so. The Help tab in the test provides detailed information about the test and its use.

Appendix 3 Measuring vocabulary size: A yes/no test of the most frequent 24,000 words of English

This test has two purposes. First, it gives teachers a chance to see the kinds of words that are high-frequency words (1,000–3,000 level), mid-frequency words (4,000–9,000 level) and low frequency words (10,000 level on). Second, you can use the test to see how big your vocabulary size is. The test will underestimate your vocabulary size because it does not provide any contexts for the words, and you do not get any credit for partial knowledge. Among the low-frequency words, there will be many you do not know. If you are an adult native speaker of English you should know somewhere approaching 20,000 words.

The activity
Can you give a meaning for each word?

1,000–2,000	3,000–4,000	5,000–6,000	7,000–8,000
base	efficient	bald	canvass
double	cite	hurdle	prerogative
hear	nuclear	sterile	constellation
paint	sin	hawk	pollen
single	exclusive	versatile	admonish
role	boxing	blog	bonanza
chat	grim	jelly	pervade
foreign	rubber	withstand	collage
rely	exotic	lettuce	sliver
bare	accustom	dove	thermometer
9,000–10,000	11,000–12,000	13,000–14,000	15,000–16,000
adrift	rune	lipoprotein	unicameral
lifeline	untoward	bogeyman	countermand
cocoon	protectorate	colossus	Valkyrie
turnip	narcissist	bipedal	decathlon
caramel	bushel	allergens	polycarbonate
terracotta	shifty	plonk	superoxide
vindictive	avarice	steeplechase	voce
maestro	snot	wayfaring	drat
coaster	stethoscope	Cyrillic	ruching
hornet	mestizo	dogwood	breadfruit

17,000–18,000	19,000–20,000	21,000–22,000	23,000–24,000
metadata	euthanise	deltic	cordgrass
intraluminal	petrodollar	kine	hade
expostulate	bumph	prograde	monos
dextrous	otiose	zoetrope	rototiller
kudu	kapok	diamine	compline
hookah	ecru	consigliere	celesta
telegenic	medicament	hibachi	ephor
histocompatibility	sinusoid	operon	hilum
ampersand	swansong	styloid	nabis
ghee	diathermy	serenata	superluminal

Each block of 10 represents 2,000 words, and so each word represents 200 words, so multiply your score by 200 to get your total vocabulary size.

Appendix 4 Guidelines for parents for helping with their child's reading and vocabulary growth

Younger children

It is helpful for young children to read their books from school out loud to someone at home. Here is a recommended procedure. Make it fun and engaging so that the child is happy to be reading with you.

It is a good idea to revisit books your child has read to and with you. Often children ask for a reread, especially when they are pre-readers. Asking for a re-read four and five times over at one sitting is not unusual for children between the ages 2 to 5 years. When a school-age child is learning to read, building fluency and confidence with words and text is an important part of their development. Re-reading is excellent for this. Make re-reading fun and lively. If the child is reluctant, 'pushing' for re-reading could well put your child off sharing reading with you.

Try to have a regular time for reading together when things are quiet. The more reading they do, the better they will become at reading. Read more complex books with them, too, following the *reading to and with* steps. Your child might want to try some of the reading. A good way is to take turns. You read some and they read what they feel they are able to read.

Steps

- Sit comfortably with your child.

    Connecting together is important for eye contact.

    Sitting strategically is important for interaction.

- Prepare for what you and your child are going to do.
- Select the book you will read together.

    The child might select one from several choices of books, or there might be a 'book to be read'.

- Get ready to start.
- Talk about the title. Read it.
- Discuss what the book might be about—*prediction and further thinking.*

- Look carefully together at the visuals.

    Visuals carry text meaning and most often help the understanding of the print.

- Talk lots together about the visuals—in detail.

    Turn-take, interact, expand, suggest, question as you move through the visuals.

    Sometimes prompt their thinking and ideas.

    Sometimes share your thinking and ideas.

    Use expression in your talk and sharing.

    Share lots—this develops text concepts and ideas, and vocabulary and expressive language.

    Recap on the book contents based on the visuals and title.

- Before reading the print as a flowing text, focus on key vocabulary in the text.

    These may be words:

    a) your child finds difficult to read and pronounce

    b) your child doesn't fully understand

    c) that are highly significant for text meaning.

- Your child could look for these words, pointing them out.
- You too can join in.
- Practise saying and reading the words you are focusing on.
- Talk about what they mean.
- Use them in sentences.

    This helps your child to gain fluency and meaning control over these words before actually reading the print text as a whole.

- Get ready to read the printed text together.

    *Focus on developing both your child's enjoyment of reading **and** ease of reading—namely that the child understands the meaning of the text, alongside becoming fluent with and understanding important vocabulary.*

    *At home, it is **very** helpful if you and other family members 'read the book' in your strongest language—which might not be English. If it* *is another language, make up a 'book text' in that language (see van Hees, 2001). This is an important stage. Book text is not just talk. It is spoken written sentences—different to conversational talk.*

- Read the print.

  Sometimes you might both read the print together.

  Sometimes you might each take turns.

  Sometimes your child might read it on his/her own.

- Predict and anticipate what's to come.
- Recall and review what's been.
- Talk as well as read.

  Get this in balance. Too much talk will stop the flow of reading, yet some talk throughout helps understanding and making sense of what you are reading together.

- When reading along:
  - *attend to the words*
  - ***flow*** *the text—reading fluency means the words 'flow along' in linked expression, even if it's read quite slowly*
  - *encourage your child to notice and follow the print*
  - *encourage your child to try*
  - *use expression.*
- Pause and prompt—*just enough. Praise and encourage* **lots**.
- If it's a struggle: model, try together, get your child to try, re-run.
- Re-read the whole text again so it is fluent and flows, and is 'easy'.
- Encourage independence when and if your child is ready.
- Recall and remember what's in the book and what the book's about—*recap*.
- Talk about and share the visual and text meaning.

  Support your child to talk and recall. Be in conversation. Give think-and-talk space for your child to speak.

  Stimulate and guide if and when needed.

- Praise and congratulate your child.
- Encourage your child to share how the reading was for him/her.

- Share your enjoyment and interest in the book.

Reading to and with an older child
- Talk about the title and what it's about.
- Read the contents page together and choose parts to read.
- Predict what the chapter or part might be about or have in it.
- Where there are diagrams or photos or pictures, talk about them, exploring what's there, but also any matters or thoughts related to them but not directly there.
- Together, talk about and share your own knowledge and experiences about the topic.
- Look up topics or ideas in the index (if it is a factual book).
- Identify and discuss any key vocabulary that is difficult, or important, or interesting.
- Use the text and your own understanding of words to explore important, or new, or difficult words. At times consult a dictionary.
- Read parts together. You take turns to read, too. Sometimes your child might read out loud to you.
- At times your child could read a part silently and then talk with you about what he/she has just read.
- Pause at a part just read and retell key ideas in what has just been read.
- Talk about what is important and why; what's interesting and why.
- Discuss together reactions and thoughts.
- At times go back to a part just read and recall or revisit it.

Most of all, make reading with an older child a positive and dynamic experience that is involving and sharing.

The reading to and with approaches explained here are proven effective ways to read to and with your child at home.

Appendix 5 A simple text marked for word frequency levels

This text has been analysed using a frequency profiler program like the one at http://www.lextutor.ca. The words not marked are in the first 1,000 words of English. These words make up most of the text. The words with {2} in front are from the second 1,000, those with {5} in front are from the fifth 1,000, and so on. There are no words from the third and fourth 1,000s, but there is one from the fifth (wee) and one from the ninth (porridge). {31} marks proper nouns, and {33} is a transparent compound (upstairs), where the word is composed of clearly related parts. Texts written for older learners have many more words beyond the first and second 1,000. Note, however, that even a very simple text like this has some lower-frequency topic words (such as *wee*, *porridge*).

The three bears

Once upon a time there were three bears. There was very big father bear. There was big mother bear and there was little {5}wee baby bear. They had three chairs. A very big chair for father bear, a big chair for mother bear and a little {5}wee chair for baby bear. They had three beds, a very big bed for father bear, a big bed for mother bear and a little {5}wee bed for baby bear. And they had three {2}bowls for {9}porridge.

One day mother bear made some {9}porridge. The {9}porridge was too hot, so they went out for a walk in the woods. {31}Goldilocks was out for a walk too. She came to the house of the three bears and she went in. She looked at the three {2}bowls of {9}porridge. She tried father bear's {9}porridge. It was too hot. She tried mother bear's {9}porridge. It was too hot too. She tried baby bear's {9}porridge. It was just right so she ate it all up.

She tried father bear's chair. It was too big. She tried mother bear's chair. It was too big too. She tried baby bear's chair. It was just right but it broke.

{31}Goldilocks went {33}upstairs. She looked at the three beds. She tried father bear's bed. It was too big. She tried mother bear's bed. It was too big too. She tried baby bear's bed. It was just right. {31}Goldilocks fell {2}asleep.

The three bears came home. Who's been eating my {9}porridge, said father bear in a very big voice. Who's been eating my {9}porridge, said mother bear in a big voice and who's been eating my {9}porridge, said baby bear in a little {5}wee voice and has eaten it all up?

Who's been sitting on my chair, said father bear in a very big voice. Who's been sitting on my chair, said mother bear in a big voice, and who's been sitting on my chair, said baby bear in a little {5}wee voice and broken it all up?

> The three bears went {33}upstairs. Who's been sleeping in my bed, said father bear in a very big voice. Who's been sleeping in my bed, said mother bear in a big voice, and who's been sleeping in my bed said baby bear in a little {5}wee voice, and look here she is. {31}Goldilocks woke up. There were the three bears looking at her. She jumped out of bed. She ran out of the house. Then she ran and ran and ran all the way home.

The WordProfiler provides the analysis this way:

Figure A9.1: Results from running a text through the Vocabprofiler program

Freq. Level	Families	Types	Tokens	Coverage%	Cum%
Kid250 - 1:	56	66	332	79.24	79.24%
Kid250 - 2:	6	8	53	12.65	91.89%
Kid250 - 3:	4	4	5	1.19	93.08%
Kid250 - 4:	1	1	9	2.15	95.23%
Kid250 - 5:				0.00	95.23%
Kid250 - 6:				0.00	95.23%
Kid250 - 7:				0.00	95.23%
Kid250 - 8:				0.00	95.23%
Kid250 - 9:				0.00	95.23%
Kid250 - 10:				0.00	95.23%
Off-List known:	2	2	16	3.82	99.05%
Off-List unknown:	?	1	4	0.95	100.00%
Total	69+?	82	419	100%	100%

Words in text (tokens):	419
Different words (types):	82
Type-token ratio:	0.20
Tokens per type:	5.11
Pertaining to onlist only	
Tokens:	415
Types:	81
Families:	69
Tokens per family:	6.01
Types per family:	1.17

Figure A9.2: Output from the Vocabprofiler program showing a text with different frequency level words marked by different colours

Integral text: once upon a time there were three bears there was very big father bear there was big mother bear and there was little wee baby bear they had three chairs a very big chair for father bear a big chair for mother bear and a little wee chair for baby bear they had three beds a very big bed for father bear a big bed for mother bear and a little wee bed for baby bear and they had three bowls for porridge one day mother bear made some porridge the porridge was too hot so they went out for a walk in the woods goldilocks was out for a walk too she came to the house of the three bears and she went in she looked at the three bowls of porridge she tried father bear porridge it was too hot she tried mother bear porridge it was too hot too she tried baby bear porridge it was just right so she ate it all up she tried father bear chair it was too big she tried mother bear chair it was too big too she tried baby bear chair it was just right but it broke goldilocks went upstairs she looked at the three beds she tried father bear bed it was too big she tried mother bear bed it was too big too she tried baby bear bed it was just right goldilocks fell asleep the three bears came home who been eating my porridge said father bear in a very big voice who been eating my porridge said mother bear in a big voice and who been eating my porridge said baby bear in a little wee voice and eaten it all up who been sitting on my chair said father bear in a very big voice who been sitting on my chair said mother bear in a big voice and who been sitting on my chair said baby bear in a little wee voice and broken it all up the three bears went upstairs who been sleeping in my bed said father bear in a very big voice who been sleeping in my bed said mother bear in a big voice and who been sleeping in my bed said baby bear in a little wee voice and look here she is goldilocks woke up there were the three bears looking at her she jumped out of bed she ran out of the house then she ran and ran and ran all the way home

Appendix 6 Steps in semantic mapping

Why do semantic mapping?

Semantic mapping helps vocabulary knowledge, text meaning-making and preparing to write.

- The more the learners work with what they are learning and reading, the more they will understand not only the words and ideas at the surface level, but also what's deeper in meaning inside the text.

- Using semantic mapping is an excellent method to use when preparing to write, because it means learners have the necessary vocabulary, ideas and knowledge, which are thought out and organised. Throughout semantic mapping, with more or less guidance, learners have talked and discussed, explained and justified, and used extended expression, and they have needed to be precise. All this provides a strong basis on which to build a written text.

- Semantic mapping is a means to organise ideas and knowledge. In oral and written presentations, deciding on a logical sequence of ideas and presenting them clearly is important.

- Semantic mapping is a great way to have learners realise they might need to investigate further what they don't know or are unsure of. The approach that follows was developed by van Hees (2002) and has proven effectiveness for vocabulary learning.

To make a semantic map using pictures

What follows are the guided steps you would take with learners, explained as if you were addressing them.

You will need: a big sheet of paper, scissors, glue, pens and pencils.

You will also need to: help each other work together, share ideas, talk and listen, write and check.

Jobs in your group—all working together:
- a person to get and collect things
- a person to make sure the group works well together
- a person who checks everything people do
- people who write the headings
- people who draw.

Steps

1. Make sure everyone has one or more jobs—so that everyone is busy, helping and working.
2. Go to a table where you will work.
3. Collect all you need from the teacher.
4. Sort out your pictures into groups. You need to talk about this in your group—decide together.
5. Make some labels for the groups of pictures you have sorted.

    You might write three different sorts of labels:
    - a one-word label (e.g. Planets)
    - a group of words that give the idea of why they are grouped this way (e.g. Planets in our solar system)
    - a sentence (e.g. These are the planets in our solar system).

1. Lay out your groups of pictures on your big sheet of paper. Put your labels with them.
2. Talk about how you would like to glue them and how to make the labels so they are easy and clear for someone else to read.
3. Talk about any extra drawings you could do for each of the groups you have made.
4. Check with the teacher every now and then about what you are doing.
5. Glue and draw and write. Do you all have a job? Are you all helping and working?
6. Make sure everything is correct and clear. Then ask the teacher to look one more time to check.
7. Talk about whether you as a group think pictures and drawings might be helpful to add in.

To make a semantic map using words

Work almost the same way as with the pictures mind map, this time using words and sorting and grouping these. You might want to put pictures and words together in a semantic map. Remember, you are making it for someone else to understand and read. If you decide to have pictures too, think about how you can use the words and pictures to make a clear semantic map for others and yourselves to understand and read.

Appendix 7 The most useful word stems

Table A7.1: The 25 most useful word stems, their meanings and words containing them

The word stem, its meaning, a high-frequency word containing it, and an example of its connection to an unfamiliar word	Mid-frequency words containing the word stem
-spec(t)-, -spic-, -scope- = "look" as in *respect* "to *look upon* somebody with admiration". A **perspective** is a particular way of *looking* at things.	aspect, inspect, prospect, suspect, spectacle, speculate, perspective, spectrum, respective, spectacular, retrospect, spectator, inspectorate, spectre, specify, specimen, despicable, conspicuous, microscope, kaleidoscope, telescope, stethoscope, sceptic*, spy*
-posit-, -pos- = "put" as in *position* "a place where somebody or something is *put*". To **pose** is to *put* somebody into a particular position to be photographed.	impose, opposite, pose, dispose, compose, deposit, expose, proposition, compost, posture, disposition, provost, superimpose, depose, repository, predispose, decompose, transpose, compound*
-vers-, -vert- = "turn" as in *reverse* "*turn* something the other way around". **Perverse** means thoroughly *turned* to the wrong way.	versus, adverse, diverse, diversify, diversion, perverse, traverse, convert, divert, inverse, revert, inadvertent, pervert, extrovert, vertebra, vertebrate, subvert, subversive
-vent-, -ven- = "come" as in *event* "the *coming* of something". A **convention** is a large meeting where people *come* together to discuss some issues.	invent, convention, advent, convent, circumvent, avenue, convenient, intervene, revenue, venue, convene, reconvene, convenor, contravene, souvenir, covenant
-ceive-, -cept- = "take" as in *accept, receive* "to *take* what is offered". To **intercept** is to *take* something when it is on its way from one place to another.	concept, intercept, deceive, deceptive, perception, perceive, reception, receipt, receiver, receptive, misconception, perceptive, receptor, misconceive, susceptible
-super- = "above" as in *super* "being *above* somebody or something". To be **supervised** is to be directed by somebody *above* you.	superb, supermarket, supervise, superior, superintendent, superficial, superman, supersede, superfluous, superstore, supernatural, superstar, superstructure, superpower, supersonic
-nam-, -nom-, -nym- = "name" as in *name*. To **nominate** is to put someone's *name* forward for election.	surname, nickname, rename, nominate, nominal, misnomer, renown, nominee, denomination, anonymous, synonym, acronym, anonymity, pseudonym, noun*
-sens-, -sent- = "feel, sense" as in *sense*. **Consent** means having the same *feelings* and opinions about something and therefore being in agreement. Sensual means of the pleasures of the *senses*.	sentence, sensible, nonsense, sensitive, sensual, sensor, scent, sensation, consensus, resent, sentiment, consent, assent, dissent
-sta-, -stan-, -stat- = "stand" as in *stand*. **Instant** means happening quickly without anything *standing* in between two events.	stable, stall, status, distant, circumstance, instant, stance, static, obstacle, stool*, statue, pedestal, stature

-mit-, -mis- = "send" as in *committee* "a group of people who are sent to be together to conduct some particular business". To *transmit* is to *send* out electric signals.	permit, transmit, submit, emit, remit, omit, message, mission, premise, dismiss, missile, submission, demise, omission
-mid-, -med(i)- = "middle" as in *middle*. *Mediocre* means being in the *middle* position ranging from good to bad.	immediate, medium, media, medieval, intermediate, Mediterranean, mediocre, mediate, meridian, meddle, median, intermediary, amid
-pris-, -pre- = "take" as in *surprise* "something which takes your attention unexpectedly". If something *comprises* a number of things, it *takes* them in as its parts.	prison, enterprise, comprise, apprentice, prey, apprehend, comprehend, predatory, entrepreneur, incomprehensible, apprehension, comprehensive, entrepreneurial
-dict-, -dicate = "say" as in *indicate* "to say something indirectly". To *dedicate* a book or an artistic work to somebody is to *say* that a book or an artistic work is issued or performed in one's honour.	dictate, dedicate, abdicate, predicate, vindicate, predict, contradict, verdict, indict, diction, ditto*, index*
-cess- = "go" as in *process* "actions *gone* through". Making a *concession* involves *going* along with somebody's opinions.	access, excess, recession, concession, recess, ancestor, predecessor, procession, succession, abscess, microprocessor, cease*
-form- = "form" as in *form*. The *format* of a book is its *form* such as its shape, size and design.	formal, perform, transform, uniform, format, conform, formula, reform, deform, formative, morphology*
-tract- = "draw" as in *attract* "to draw attention". To *extract* is to *draw* something out.	extract, distract, abstract, subtract, detract, retract, contraction, protracted, traction, tractor, intractable
-graph- = "write" as in *paragraph* "a written passage". A *telegraph* is sending *written* messages using radio signals.	telegraph, autobiography, biography, pornography, autograph, biographer, typographical, graph, graphic, topography, demography, geography
-gen- = "produce" as in *generate* "*produce*". *Genes* are part of a cell that *produce* similar features in children.	genuine, gene, genesis, genetic, genius, indigenous, ingenuity, engender, congenital, genital, ingenious
-duce-, -duct- = "lead" as in *introduce/introduction* "*leading* something/somebody into a place, condition or circle of people". To *induce* is to *lead* somebody to do something unwise.	induce, deduce, seduce, conducive, conduct, abduct, viaduct, aqueduct, superconductor, subdue*
-voca-, -vok- is a variation of -voic- = "voice" as in *voice*. To *advocate* is to *voice* one's opinions publicly to support something.	advocate, vocabulary, vocal, invoke/invocation, equivocal, evoke/evocation, vowel, advocacy

-cis-, -cid- = "cut" as in *decide/decision* "a judgement about where to cut off (what to do or not to do). To *excise* is to remove by *cutting* something out.	precise, excise, circumcise, concise, incise, scissors, suicide, pesticide
-pla- is a variant of -fla- = "flat" as in *flat*. A *plaice* is a *flat* sea fish.	plain, plane, plate, plaice, plateau, plot*, flounder*
-sec-, -sequ- = "follow" as in *second* "*following the first*". A *consequence* is what *follows* as an effect.	consequence, sequence, subsequent, consecutive, sequel, prosecute, consequential
-for(t)- = "strong" as in *force*. A *fortress* is a very *strong* building for protecting people.	fortress, fortified, fortitude, comfort, effort, fort, enforce, reinforce, forte
-vis- = "see" as in *visit* "go to see someone". Something *visible* can be *seen*.	visible, envisage, revise, supervise, visual, vision, television

Note: The words with the * mark show variations in form.

In the row for *-for(t)*, at the bottom of the table, we can see that the stem takes two forms: for, fort. Its meaning, *strong*, is given in quotation marks and *force* is a word from the most frequent 2,000 words of English containing the stem. The example mid-frequency word *fortress*, which happens to be the first of the words given in column 2 of the table, is followed by an explanation or hint that shows how the meaning of -fort- is related to the meaning of *fortress*. Any of the words in column 2 could have a similar hint to help learning. For example, *fortitude* is the strength to continue doing something. *Effort* is the amount of strength needed to do something. All the words in column 2 are from the 3rd to 10th 1,000 words of English. The data in column 1, with appropriate changes to the example, could be included in a dictionary entry for each of the words in column 2.

Table A7.2: Alphabetically arranged stems that are in at least 5 words (not including the stems listed in Table A7.1)

-ag- *agent, agitate* (act)	-gress- *progress, regress* (step)	-port- *transport, report* (carry)
-angl- *angle, ankle, anchor*	-hibit-, -habit- *prohibit* (hold)	-prec-, -pr-/z/- *price, prize* (value)
-aster-, -astro- *disaster* (star)	-hum(an)- *human, humble*	-prim- *prime, primary* (first)
-audi-, *audience* (listen)	-ject- *reject, objective* (throw)	-publi(c)- *public, publish*
-b-l- *ball, bulge, bulk, belly*	-join-, -junct- *join, juncture*	-puls- *pulse, compulsion* (push)
-b-n-, *benefit, bonus, bounty*	-jud-, -jur- *judgement, jury*	-quali- *quality, qualify, quasi*
br- *brand, brew, brood* (heat)	-c-n- *can, cunning, keen* (know)	-(re)lat- *relate, collate, atlas*
-car-, *carry, cargo, caravan*	-leg- *legal, privilege* (law)	-sal-, -sau- *salt, salad, sauce*
-cav-, ca- *cave, cabinet* (hollow)	-like- *like, alike, unlike, likeness*	-scal-, -scend- *scale* (climb)
-ced-, -ceed- *proceed* (go)	-lit- *letter, obliterate, literate*	-sec-, -sequ- *second* (follow)
-ceive-, -cept- *accept* (receive)	-locate, -local- *local* (place)	-sect-, -seg- *section, insect*
-cent- *accent* (emphasis)	-long- *long, length, prolong*	-sed-, -sid- *reside* (settle)
-cess- *process, access* (go)	-ma(g)- *magnificent* (important)	-sens-, -sent- *sense, sentence*
-chemist-, -chemical *chemical*	-ma(j)- *major* (important_	-sent-, -senc- *sense, resent* (feel)
-cis-, -cid- *decide* (cut)	-man-, -main- *remain* (stay)	-serv- *service, deserve* (do)
-clam-, -claim- *claim* (say)	-mar-, -mer- *market* (trade)	-sim-, -sem- *similar, assemble*
-clus- , -clud- *include* (close)	-memor- *memory* (remember)	-soci(al)- *social, socialism*
-corp- *corporation* (body)	-meter *meter* (measure)	-sound-, -son- *sound, consonant*
-course-, -co(ur)- *course* (run)	-mil(li)- *million* (thousand)	-/s/pir- *spirit, expire* (breath)
-cur- *secure, accurate* (care)	-min(im)- *minimum* (small)	-sti- *stick(vb), distinct, stitch*
-cur(s)- *current, cursor* (run)	-m-n- *mind, monument, mental*	-struct- *structure, construct*
-dom- *control* (dominate)	-neg- *neglect, renege, negate* (not)	-syn- *system, syndrome, synthesis*
-electr-*electricity*	-nerv-, -neuro- *nerve*	-tele- *television, telex* (far)
-equa-, -equi- *equal, equivalent*	-not- *note, notion, annotate* (idea)	-ten- *tend, tense, tent* (stretch)
-fa- *fame, infant, fable* (speak)	-nounc- *announce* (say)	-ten-, -tent- *contents* (hold)
-fer- *offer, confer* (bring)	-num- *number, enumerate*	-tent-, -tain- *maintain* (keep)
-fin- *finish, define* (limit)	-par- *compare, par, parity, peer*	-term- *term, exterminate* (end)
-flo-r- *flower, flour, flourish*	-part- *part, partner, particle*	-val(u)- *value, valid, equivalent*
-flu- *influence, fluid* (flow)	-pel- *appeal, propel* (force)	-vid-, -vis- *divide, divisive*
-gl- *glass, glitter* (shine)	-pend- *depend, pendulum* (hang)	-voca-, -vok- *voice, invoke*
-gno- *know, diagnose* (ignore)	-pla-, plea- *please, complacent*	-wr-n-, -wor- *worry, wrinkle,* (twist)
-grad- *grade, gradual* (degree)	-plant- *plant, transplant, implant*	
-f(-)a(c)- *fact, manufacture* (do)	-p-n- *pain, penalty, punish*	

Table A7.2 contains almost 100 word stems, which are the most useful ones after those in Table A7.1. Each stem occurs in at least five mid-frequency words. The word in italics is a high-frequency word containing the stem, and the word in brackets is the meaning of the stem. Where the first example and the meaning are the same, only one is given, for example -car-, *carry*. Where there is space in the table, extra examples are given; so in the entry for -pla-, plea-, the most common word is *please* and the meaning of the stems is 'please', and *complacent* is a low-frequency example.

The data in this appendix are taken from Wei and Nation (2013).

Appendix 8 The most useful prefixes and suffixes

Following is a sequenced list of derivational affixes for learners of English.

Stage 1
-able, -er, -ish, -less, -ly, -ness, -th, -y, non-, un-

Stage 2
-al, -ation, -ess, -ful, -ism, -ist, -ity, -ize, -ment, -ous, in-

Stage 3
-age (leakage), -al (arrival), -ally (idiotically), -an (American), -ance (clearance), -ant (consultant), -ary (revolutionary), -atory (confirmatory), -dom (kingdom; officialdom), -eer (black marketeer), -en (wooden), -en (widen), -ence (emergence), -ent (absorbent), -ery (bakery; trickery), -ese (Japanese; officialese), -esque (picturesque), -ette (usherette; roomette), -hood (childhood), -i (Israeli), -ian (phonetician; Johnsonian), -ite (Paisleyite; also chemical meaning), -let (coverlet), -ling (duckling), -ly (leisurely), -most (topmost), -ory (contradictory), -ship (studentship), -ward (homeward), -ways (crossways), -wise (endwise; discussion-wise), anti- (anti-inflation), ante- (anteroom), arch- (archbishop), bi- (biplane), circum- (circumnavigate), counter- (counter-attack), en- (encage; enslave), ex- (ex-president), fore- (forename), hyper- (hyperactive), inter- (inter-African, interweave), mid- (mid-week), mis- (misfit), neo- (neo-colonialism), post- (post-date), pro- (pro-British), semi- (semi-automatic), sub- (subclassify; subterranean), un- (untie; unburden).

Stage 4
-able, -ee, -ic, -ify, -ion, -ist, -ition, -ive, -th, -y, pre-, re-.

Stage 5
-ar (circular), -ate (compassionate; captivate; electorate), -et (packet, casket), -some (troublesome), -ure (departure, exposure), ab-, ad-, com-, de-, dis-, ex- (out), in- (in), ob-, per-, pro- (in front of), trans-.

Appendix 9 *Steps for word experts*

Write the word down and notice how it is written.

1. Write out the sentence from the text that has the word in it or recall the word as it was used when you heard it.
2. Write down what you think is the word's meaning. If you are unsure, make an informed guess. Try to make your explanation or meaning clear and exact.
3. Write out your own sentence using the word and try to show you understand the word.
4. Look up the word in one or more dictionaries to find out how the meaning is explained in these dictionaries. Write out the definition or explanations from each dictionary.
5. Go back to your sentence at 3. Now try to write out even better sentences that show that you understand the meaning.
6. Draw a simple drawing for the word to help you remember the word, what it is or what it means.

My word experts learning sheet

1. The word—in English and in my other language/s:

2. The sentence from the text with the word:

3. What I/we think the word means—our explanation:

4. My/our sentences using the word:

5. Explanations/definitions in the dictionaries:

6. My/our second set of sentences using the word:

7. A drawing to help me remember the word:

Appendix 10 *A test of "What every primary teacher should know about vocabulary"*

Multiple-choice test

1. What is the most important condition for vocabulary learning?
   A   multiple encounters
   B   varied use
   C   elaboration
   D   retrieval

2. What percentage coverage of the vocabulary of a reading text is needed for most learners to gain good unassisted comprehension?
   A   78%
   B   80%
   C   90%
   D   98%

3. Words that make up a lexical set, like the names of fruit such as *banana, apple, plum, peach, pear,* are best learned initially by:
   A   contrasting them with each other
   B   putting them in a context like buying fruit at the market
   C   looking at the relationships between them
   D   keeping them widely separated from each other

4. On average, how many words do native speakers acquire per year in the first 20 years of their life?
   A   100
   B   1,000
   C   5,000
   D   10,000

5. A collocation is two or more words that:
   A   have a different meaning from the sum of their parts
   B   have related meanings
   C   are always in a fixed order
   D   often occur near each other

6. Which of these most helps vocabulary learning?
   A   meeting or using the word in a new way
   B   having its meaning explained
   C   meeting the word in context
   D   searching for the word in a dictionary

7. Explanations of unknown words are most effective if:
   A they are short and precise
   B they contain plenty of useful detail
   C they are written as complete sentences
   D they are accompanied by grammatical information

8. Quickly providing meanings for unknown words while listening or reading:
   A has little effect on comprehension of the text
   B upsets comprehension of the text
   C greatly increases the amount of vocabulary learned
   D results in little vocabulary learning

9. Retrieval involves:
   A receptive learning
   B productive learning
   C recalling an item
   D recognising that two given items go together

10. Receptive knowledge is the kind of knowledge needed for:
    A meeting new words
    B analysing new words
    C speaking and writing
    D listening and reading

11. Which one of these sets contains words that will be easier to learn at the same time?
    A avocado, persimmon, pomegranate, mangosteen
    B stubborn, willing, exhausted, refreshed
    C terrified, horrified, aghast, petrified
    D flee, terrified, companion, refuge

12. How many high-frequency words are there in English?
    A 9,000
    B 5,000
    C 3,000
    D 1,000

13. A 7-year-old native speaker of English is likely to know:
    A all the high-frequency words
    B all the high- and mid-frequency words
    C all the low-frequency words
    D all the high-, mid-, and low-frequency words

Appendix 10 A test of "What every primary teacher should know about vocabulary"

14. The Picture Vocabulary Size Test measures knowledge of:
    A   the most frequent 96 words of English
    B   the first 1,000 words of English
    C   the mid-frequency words
    D   the most frequent 6,000 words of English

15. The principle of the four strands says that:
    A   each lesson should spend equal time on meaning-focused input, meaning-focused output, language-focused learning and fluency development
    B   a well-balanced course should have four equal strands of meaning-focused input, meaning-focused output, language-focused learning and fluency development
    C   a language course should include listening, speaking, reading and writing
    D   language learning needs the four strands of noticing, retrieval, elaboration and repetition

16. A word family contains:
    A   all the meanings of a word
    B   a word, its opposites and its strong associates
    C   all its parts of speech
    D   a word form and its closely related inflected and derived forms

17. Which of these is a derived form of the word *mend*?
    A   mends
    B   unmendable
    C   mending
    D   mend meaning *improve*, as in "mend your ways"

18. Word consciousness is:
    A   an activity for teaching receptive vocabulary
    B   an interest in words and how to learn them
    C   an essential condition for learning vocabulary
    D   knowledge of word forms

19. For young native speakers, most vocabulary learning occurs:
    A   as a result of vocabulary teaching in school
    B   through wide reading
    C   through parents and family members teaching words
    D   through a variety of experiences with language

20. Morphological problem solving involves:
    A   understanding words through knowledge of their parts
    B   learning spelling rules
    C   guessing words from a variety of context clues
    D   group discussion

21. Productive knowledge is the kind of knowledge needed for:
    A   meeting new words
    B   analysing new words
    C   speaking and writing
    D   listening and reading

22. Each year young native speakers with the smallest vocabulary sizes for their age learn around:
    A   50 words
    B   100 words
    C   500 words
    D   1,000 words

23. The average 5-year-old native speaker beginning school knows around:
    A   500 words
    B   1,000 words
    C   3,000 words
    D   5,000 words

24. For young children, the learning of words is most affected by:
    A   multiple encounters and the quality of the meetings
    B   reading
    C   vocabulary teaching
    D   word consciousness

25. Children of the same age tend to learn the same words because:
    A   they are taught the same words
    B   they read the same books
    C   schools follow similar syllabuses
    D   learning is affected by frequency of meetings with the words

26. Words in the same word family differ from each other in that:
    A   they have different meanings
    B   they have different prefixes and suffixes
    C   they need to be learned separately
    D   they are borrowed from different languages

Appendix 10 A test of "What every primary teacher should know about vocabulary"

27. In any text, half of the different words:
    A   occur only once
    B   occur very frequently
    C   are specialised words
    D   are mid-frequency words

28. The most important thing a teacher can do to help learners increase their vocabulary is to:
    A   make sure they do lots of reading and engage with quality spoken language
    B   teach them lots of words
    C   get them to do lots of vocabulary-focused activities
    D   teach them dictionary use skills

29. The most useful way in which teachers can give deliberate attention to vocabulary is to:
    A   get the learners doing vocabulary activities like crossword puzzles and word finder
    B   train the learners in dictionary use
    C   focus on words in the context of content-focused learning
    D   do activities to develop word consciousness

30. In a school year by reading for around 4 hours a week, learners could read texts totaling in length:
    A   10,000 words
    B   50,000 words
    C   100,000 words
    D   1,000,000 words

31. The rule of thumb for estimating vocabulary size:
    A   involves looking at a table of norms
    B   requires the use of a calculator
    C   requires you to know the child's age
    D   depends on the child's score on the Picture Vocabulary Size Test

32. Each word tested on the Picture Vocabulary Size Test represents:
    A   just over 60 words
    B   100 words
    C   600 words
    D   1,000 words

171

33. In order to already be familiar with 98% of the words in a school reading text, a child would need to know around:
    A   1,000 words
    B   3,000 words
    C   6,000 words
    D   9,000 words

34. To close the gap between children with the lower vocabulary sizes for their age and children with average vocabulary sizes, those with the lower vocabulary sizes would need to learn an additional:
    A   word a day
    B   three words a day
    C   five words a day
    D   10 words a day

35. An interview test of vocabulary requires the learner to:
    A   choose the right answer
    B   recall the form of the word
    C   explain the meaning of a word
    D   all the above

36. Varied use involves:
    A   retrieval
    B   meeting or using the word in new contexts
    C   previous knowledge of the word
    D   all of the above

37. Pause, prompt, praise involves:
    A   vocabulary study
    B   the teaching of new words
    C   providing spelling rules
    D   giving the learner a chance to provide the answer

38. Breaking a word into word parts and relating the parts to the meaning is an example of the learning condition of:
    A   noticing
    B   repetition
    C   varied use
    D   elaboration

Appendix 10 A test of "What every primary teacher should know about vocabulary"

39. Looking up a word in the dictionary is an example of the learning condition of:
    A retrieval
    B varied use
    C deliberate learning
    D noticing

40. What is the most important condition affecting vocabulary learning?
    A retrieval
    B repetition
    C varied use
    D deliberate attention

41. Final silent *e*:
    A affects the spelling but not the pronunciation of words
    B is related to the pronunciation of the previous vowel
    C involves checked sounds
    D is part of a very regular spelling rule.

42. Which of these pairs are homonyms?
    A eye—I
    B bread—bred
    C bowl (a ball)—bowl (a container)
    D sweet (taste)—sweet (face)

43. What is involved in the word part strategy?
    A finding the word parts in a word
    B connecting new knowledge to previous knowledge
    C relating the meanings of the parts to the meaning of the word
    D all the above

44. A collocation is:
    A a special meaning of a word that is not related to its core meaning
    B the parts of a word
    C two or more words that often occur together
    D all the above

45. How many true idioms are there in English?
    A 100
    B 1,000
    C 10,000
    D 100,000

173

46. Meaning-focused input involves:
    A   reading and listening to texts at the right level
    B   listening to words being explained
    C   looking up words in a dictionary
    D   all the above

47. Receptive knowledge is the kind of knowledge needed for:
    A   meeting new words
    B   analysing new words
    C   speaking and writing
    D   listening and reading

48. Preteaching vocabulary before reading a text:
    A   usually improves comprehension of the text
    B   is not needed if there is preteaching of content
    C   usually improves comprehension if it is accompanied by preteaching of content
    D   only helps comprehension if a lot of time is spent on the preteaching

49. For young native speakers, most vocabulary learning occurs:
    A   as a result of vocabulary teaching in school
    B   through wide reading
    C   through parents and family members teaching words
    D   through a variety of experiences with language

50. The different senses of a word in a dictionary:
    A   are different words
    B   all share the same core meaning
    C   need to be learned at the same time
    D   have different etymologies

Appendix 10 A test of "What every primary teacher should know about vocabulary"

Brief answer test

1. List the four strands.
2. What are the six conditions favouring vocabulary learning?
3. Draw on the conditions for learning in order to explain how reading helps vocabulary learning.
4. Explain what happens in *pause, prompt, praise*.
5. Describe the rule of thumb for estimating a child's vocabulary size.
6. Suggest three ways to use a reading text to help vocabulary learning.
7. List three arguments for and three arguments against direct vocabulary teaching.
8. Describe three ways of giving attention to the form of a word.
9. Explain the 'depth of processing' principle, giving an example.
10. Explain what word consciousness is, and name four word consciousness activities.
11. Explain the free and checked sounds rule with examples.
12. What are homonyms, homophones and homographs?
13. Apply the word part strategy to this word: *inspector*.
14. Explain how *special, spectator* and *inspector* are related to each other.
15. Explain the difference between core meaning and word senses, using *green* as an example.
16. Explain the difference between a figurative and an idiom. Give examples.
17. What is a concordance and how can you quickly make one?
18. What is Zipf's Law and how does it apply to the teaching and learning of vocabulary?
19. Describe the word experts activity (also called word detectives or word catchers).
20. What is meaning-focused input?

References

Anthony, L. and Nation, I.S.P. (2017). *PVST* (Version 1.0.0) [Computer Software]. Tokyo, Japan: Waseda University. Available from http:// www.laurenceanthony.net/

Biemiller, A. (2005). Size and sequence in vocabulary development. In E. H. Hiebert & M. L. Kamil (Eds.), *Teaching and learning vocabulary: Bringing research into practice* (pp. 223-242). Mahwah, NJ: Lawrence Erlbaum Associates.

Biemiller, A., & Slonim, N. (2001). Estimating root word vocabulary growth in normative and advantaged populations: Evidence for a common sequence of vocabulary acquisition. *Journal of Educational Psychology, 93*(3), 498-520.

Coxhead, A. (Ed.) (2014). *New ways in teaching vocabulary*. Alexandria, VA: TESOL Press.

Farkas, G., & Beron, K. (2004). The detailed age trajectory of oral vocabulary knowledge: differences by class and race. *Social Science Research, 33*, 464–497.

McKay, P. (2006). *Assessing young language learners*. Cambridge, UK: Cambridge University Press.

Nation, I. S. P. (2013a). *Learning vocabulary in another language*. (2nd ed.). Cambridge, UK: Cambridge University Press.

Nation, P. (2013b). *What should every ESL teacher know?* Seoul: Compass Publishing.

Nation, I. S. P. (2014). How much input do you need to learn the most frequent 9,000 words? *Reading in a Foreign Language, 26*(2), 1-16.

van Hees, J. (1999). *Diagnostic oracy and literacy assessment in the four modes of listening, speaking, reading and writing*. Auckland: Auckland UniServices Ltd.

van Hees. J. (2001). The reading partnership: https://www.youtube.com/watch?v=-ycT37Y8kNQ&feature=youtu.be

van Hees, J. (2007). *Expanding oral language in the classroom*. Wellington: NZCER Press.

van Hees, J. (2014). Collective gifting and sharing. In A. Coxhead (Ed.), *New ways in teaching vocabulary* (revised), (pp. 16–18). Annapolis, MA: TESOL Press.

Wei, Z., & Nation, P. (2013). The word part technique: A very useful vocabulary teaching technique. *Modern English Teacher, 22*(1), 12-16.

White, T. G., Graves, M. F., & Slater, W. H. (1990). Growth of reading vocabulary in diverse elementary schools: Decoding and word meaning. *Journal of Educational Psychology, 82*(2), 281-290.

Bibliography

Bauer, L., & Nation, I. S. P. (1993). Word families. *International Journal of Lexicography, 6*(4), 253-279.

Biemiller, E. (2004). Teaching vocabulary in the primary grades: Vocabulary instruction needed. In J. F. Baumann & E. J. Kame'enui (Eds.), *Vocabulary instruction: Research to practice* (pp. 28-40). New York, NY: Guilford Press.

Boers, F., Eyckmans, J., & Stengers, H. (2007). Presenting figurative idioms with a touch of etymology: More than mere mnemonics? *Language Teaching Research, 11*(1), 43-62.

Carver, R. P. (1994). Percentage of unknown vocabulary words in text as a function of the relative difficulty of the text: Implications for instruction. *Journal of Reading Behavior, 26*(4), 413-437.

Coxhead, A. (2004). Using a class vocabulary box: How, why, when, where and who. *Guidelines, 26*(2), 19-23.

Coxhead, A., Nation, P., & Sim, D. (2015). The vocabulary size of native speakers of English in New Zealand secondary schools. *New Zealand Journal of Educational Studies, 50*(1), 121-135.

Elley, W. B. (1989). Vocabulary acquisition from listening to stories. *Reading Research Quarterly, 24*(2), 174-187.

Elley, W. B., & Mangubhai, F. (1981). *The impact of a book flood in Fiji primary schools*. Wellington: New Zealand Council for Educational Research.

Farkas, G., & Beron, K. (2004). The detailed age trajectory of oral vocabulary knowledge: differences by class and race. *Social Science Research, 33*, 464-497.

Halliday, M. A. K. (1985). *Spoken and written language*. Waum Ponds, VIC: Deakin University.

Hoff, E. (2006). How social contexts support and shape language development. *Developmental Review, 26*(1), 55-88.

Hu, M., & Nation, I. S. P. (2000). Vocabulary density and reading comprehension. *Reading in a Foreign Language, 13*(1), 403-430.

Laufer, B., & Nation, P. (1999). A vocabulary size test of controlled productive ability. *Language Testing, 16*(1), 36-55.

Macalister, J. (1999). School Journals and TESOL: An evaluation of the reading difficulty of School Journals for second and foreign language learners. *New Zealand Studies in Applied Linguistics, 5*, 61-85.

Martinez, R., & Schmitt, N. (2012). A phrasal expressions list. *Applied Linguistics, 33*(3), 299–320.

Marulis, L. M., & Neuman, S. B. (2010). The effects of vocabulary intervention on young children's word learning: A meta-analysis. *Review of Educational Research, 80*(3), 300–335.

McKay, P. (2006). *Assessing young language learners.* Cambridge, UK: Cambridge University Press.

Nation, I. S. P. (1993). Measuring readiness for simplified material: A test of the first 1,000 words of English. In M. L. Tickoo (Ed.), *Simplification: Theory and application.* RELC Anthology Series no. 31 (pp. 193–203). Singapore: SEAMEO-RELC.

Nation, I. S. P. (2000). Learning vocabulary in lexical sets: Dangers and guidelines. *TESOL Journal, 9*(2), 6–10.

Nation, I. S. P. (2006). How large a vocabulary is needed for reading and listening? *Canadian Modern Language Review, 63*(1), 59–82.

Nation, I. S. P. (2007). The four strands. *Innovation in Language Learning and Teaching, 1*(1), 1–12.

Nation, I. S. P. (2008). *Teaching vocabulary: Strategies and techniques.* Boston, MA: Heinle Cengage Learning. Nation, I. S. P. (2009). *Teaching ESL/EFL reading and writing.* New York, NY: Routledge.

Nation, I. S. P., & Webb, S. (2011). *Researching and analyzing vocabulary.* Boston, MA: Heinle Cengage Learning.

Schmitt, N., Jiang, X., & Grabe, W. (2011). The percentage of words known in a text and reading comprehension. *The Modern Language Journal, 95*(1), 26–43.

Scott, J. A., & Nagy, W. E. (2004). Developing word consciousness. In J. F. Baumann & E. J. Kame'enui (Eds.), *Vocabulary instruction: Research to practice* (pp. 201–217). New York, NY: Guilford Press.

Sorell, C. J. (2012). Zipf's law and vocabulary. In C. A. Chapelle (Ed.), *Encyclopaedia of applied linguistics.* Oxford, UK: Wiley-Blackwell. http://onlinelibrary.wiley.com/doi/10.1002/9781405198431.wbeal1302/abstract

Stahl, S. A., Hare, V. C., Sinatra, R., & Gregory, J. F. (1991). Defining the role of prior knowledge and vocabulary in reading comprehension: The retiring of number 41. *Journal of Reading Behavior, 23*(4), 487–508.

Stahl, S. A., & Vancil, S. J. (1986). Discussion is what makes semantic maps work in vocabulary instruction. *The Reading Teacher, 40*(1), 62–67.

van Hees, J. (1999). *Diagnostic oracy and literacy assessment in the four modes of listening, speaking, reading and writing.* Auckland: Auckland UniServices.

van Hees, J. (2000). *The home-school partnership manual and resources.* Wellington: Learning Media.

van Hees. J. (2001). The reading partnership: https://www.youtube.com/watch?v=-ycT37Y8kNQ&feature=youtube

van Hees, J. (2002). *Language teaching approaches.* Unpublished resources, University of Auckland.

van Hees, J. (2004). Partnerships at the interface: Classroom, whānau and community-based language and learning, for linguistically and culturally diverse learners. In *Language acquisition research* (pp. 81–113). An Occasional Publication. Wellington: Research Division, Ministry of Education.

van Hees, J. (2011). *Oral expression of five and six year olds in low-socio economic schools.* Auckland: The University of Auckland. ResearchSpace@Auckland

van Hees, J. (2014). Collecting gifting and sharing vocabulary. In A. Coxhead (ed.) *New ways in teaching vocabulary.* (pp. 16-18). Alexandria, VA: TESOL.

Webb, S., & Macalister, J. (2013). Is text written for children useful for L2 extensive reading? *TESOL Quarterly, 47*(2), 300–322.

Webb, S., & Nation, I. S. P. (2017). *How vocabulary is learned.* Oxford, UK: Oxford University Press.

Webb, S., & Rodgers, M. P. H. (2009). The lexical coverage of movies. *Applied Linguistics, 30*(3), 407–427.

Webb, S., & Rodgers, M. P. H. (2009). The vocabulary demands of television programs. *Language Learning, 59*(2), 335–366.

Index

alliteration 108
AntConc 113
AntWordProfiler 17
associated words 86, 134–35
   see also WordPlosion
audio-books 58, 59
audio-only texts 52–54, 123, 125

Biemiller, Andrew 25–26, 27, 30, 37
brainstorming, group 137–39

children's books and vocabulary learning 65–68
children's stories, words likely to appear 15
class discussion 87–88, 126–27
collocation 23, 80–81, 107, 121
comprehension skills 129
concordances 112–14
contexts of vocabulary knowledge and learning 19–20, 38, 39, 70, 79, 89, 91, 92, 139
   elaboration 45
   guessing from 21, 24, 30, 31, 32, 82, 85
   noticing 42
   productive use of new contexts 39–40, 127
   WordPlosion 133, 134
conversations 2, 5, 27, 28, 39, 42, 45, 48–49, 58, 61, 71, 73, 123
   culture of conversation 125
   examples of exchanges 50–51
core meaning 39, 82, 96, 97, 98, 99, 118–19, 126, 133–34
culturally influenced usage 109
cutting-edge vocabulary 125, 127, 128

deliberate attention
   analysing deliberate learning activities 86–94
   dictionary use 39, 100
   independent reading 64
   intensive reading 64, 127
   quick attention 81, 126
   reading to learners with small vocabulary size 124
   in semantic mapping 93
   shared reading 62
   spelling 118
   teachers 94
   word consciousness 97
   word knowledge and learning 20, 21, 23, 28, 38, 39, 40, 41–42, 43, 45, 66, 67, 70, 72, 76, 79–81, 84, 142
deliberate teaching 28, 76, 84, 86–94, 118
depth-of-processing principle 86, 87
dictionary use 20, 21, 24, 39, 42, 63, 68, 70, 82, 85, 88, 98, 125, 139
   activity 99–101
   poor spellers' dictionary 101
   by word experts 118, 119, 165, 166
digital material 4, 54, 62, 79
discussion 5, 39, 42, 44, 45, 55, 56, 62, 70, 77, 84, 85, 86, 104, 108, 126, 127, 130, 136
   brainstorming 137–39
   class discussion 87–88, 90, 100, 126–27
   high-frequency vocabulary 140, 141
   intensive reading 64, 88, 89
   parents 151, 154
   semantic mapping 92, 93, 157
   shared reading 59, 60, 61, 62
   word consciousness 99

elaboration 39, 40, 41, 43, 45, 66, 67, 79, 84, 90, 93, 94, 142
   examples 45–46
   oral language 49–51
   shared reading 62
English as a second or foreign language 1–2, 11, 30–31, 68, 123, 131
etymology 82, 96, 106, 118

families *see* parents and families
figuratives 107–08, 121
fluency development 22, 39, 42, 43, 59–61, 62, 63, 76, 118, 129–30, 139
   reading 62, 63–64, 65, 66, 68, 72, 124, 127, 128
focus principle 86, 87, 89
form 18, 19, 44, 126
   teaching techniques 80, 82, 85, 87
   word wall 90, 91
formative evidence 5
four strands 22, 23, 24, 42, 68, 118
   see also fluency development; language-focused learning; meaning-focused input; meaning-focused output
frequency 109–10
   see also high-frequency words; low-frequency words; mid-frequency words; word families; word family lists
   activity 110
   frequency count 7, 9–10, 17, 110
   frequency lists 9–11, 27, 110
   simple text marked for word frequency levels 155–56
Frequency program 17, 96, 110

Goldilocks zone 9, 11, 24, 29, 44, 49, 78, 94, 123, 124, 126, 135
guessing words
   from context 21, 24, 30, 31, 32, 82, 85
   from visuals 65, 129

head words 12, 23
high-frequency words 7, 8, 10, 13, 14, 15, 16, 19, 27, 29, 51, 70, 72, 92, 103, 118, 149
   activity 143–44
   containing most useful word stems 162–63
   word-focused rich instruction 139–42
homographs 111
homonyms 111–12
homophones 111, 112

idioms 107
incidental learning 11, 23, 24, 41, 42, 70, 76, 78, 86
independent reading 2, 62, 63, 64, 66, 68, 72, 127, 128, 130
intensive reading 58–59, 62, 63, 64, 68, 72, 85, 127–28, 130, 131
   activity 88–89, 106–07
   focuses and techniques 129
interference 85–86, 95
internet 4, 54–55, 71
interview tests 29–30

knowing a word 18–22, 23, 91, 124, 132
   see also form; meaning; use of words; vocabulary learning; word experts
   partial knowledge 79, 81

language-focused learning 22, 23, 42,
    68, 76, 118, 127, 129, 130
learning talk 21
learning vocabulary *see* vocabulary
    learning
lemmas 16
lexical sets 85–86, 95
linked skills activities 3, 21, 45, 67, 73,
    74, 130
listening
    audio-only texts 52–54
    digital sources 4
    high-frequency words 19
    increasing subject-related
        listening 77–78
    low-frequency words 10
    mid-frequency words 8, 19
    receptive knowledge 4, 7, 23, 33,
        39, 40, 41, 43, 44, 45, 68
    vocabulary learning 3, 5, 12,
        20–21, 23, 24, 27, 28, 39, 40, 42,
        44, 48, 71–72, 73, 127, 129, 130
    word families 12, 19
low-frequency words 7, 8, 9, 10, 11,
    13, 14, 15, 16, 20, 27, 29, 71, 149
    activity 143–44
    effect of not knowing 14, 69

meaning 18, 19, 70, 165, 166
    core meaning 39, 82, 96, 97, 98,
        99, 118–19, 126, 133–34
    guessing from context 21, 24, 30,
        31, 32, 82, 85
    oral language 72
    reading for meaning 59–61, 62,
        63, 66, 68, 85
    teaching techniques 41–42, 79–80,
        82, 87
    word families 12, 13

word wall 90, 91, 92
meaning-focused input 22, 24, 42, 76,
    118, 127, 128, 130
meaning-focused output 22, 24, 42,
    76, 118, 128–29, 130
memory tricks 119, 120
mid-frequency words 7, 8, 9, 13, 14, 15,
    16, 19, 27, 71, 83, 94, 103, 149
    activity 143–44
    containing most useful word
        stems 159–63
morphological problem solving 105
movie clips 54–55, 71
    enhancing vocabulary learning
        experience 55–57
multi-media oral language
    sources 54–57
multiple encounters 2, 38, 39, 40, 41,
    66–67, 70–71, 72, 73, 79, 127
    teaching 79, 83–84

narrow reading 63, 73
noticing 38, 39, 40, 41, 42–43, 62,
    79, 83, 84, 89, 90, 93, 94, 100,
    125, 126, 142

oral language 8, 18, 19, 20, 22–23,
    33, 130
    see also conversations
    analysing 33–36
    audio-only texts 52–54, 123, 125
    examples of sources 51–54, 71–72
    multi-media sources 54–57
    and vocabulary learning 5, 28, 39,
        40, 43, 44, 48–50, 67, 70, 71–72,
        73, 78, 87, 123, 124, 128

pair reading 63, 83, 88, 89
parents and families

guidelines for helping with reading
and vocabulary growth 151–54
learners' vocabulary at home 33, 72
reading at home 4, 61, 73, 128,
130, 151–54
participation 5, 21, 38, 39, 41, 61, 133
pause, prompt and praise 43, 128, 153
Peabody Picture Vocabulary Test 30
phonics 23
Picture Vocabulary Size Test 5, 8–9,
27, 30–31, 36, 37, 124, 145–48
increasing validity through test
administration 148
interpreting results 148
positive approach to results 147
picture vocabulary tests 30
prefixes 8, 12, 18, 21, 22, 23, 24, 80,
102–03, 105, 121
most useful prefixes and
suffixes 164
two lists of useful prefixes for
learning 103–04
pre-teaching before reading 21,
84–85, 89
productive knowledge 18, 23, 39–41,
61–62, 68, 91
assessing 33–36
attention 40
elaboration 40, 45
multiple encounters 40, 41, 66–67,
127
noticing 40, 42–43
retrieval 40, 42, 43–44, 119, 120
varied use 40, 44–45, 61–62, 64,
94
productive skills 40
Project Gutenberg 110
pronunciation 20, 35, 40, 80, 82, 100,
111

checked sounds 116
free sounds 116
spelling–sound
correspondence 116–18, 121–22
proper nouns 13, 14, 16, 69
punctuation 129
pyramid procedure 90

quick attention or glossing 81, 126

radio broadcasts 72
text analysis 52–54
Range program 17
reading
see also independent reading;
intensive reading; re-reading;
shared or guided reading
children's books 65–68
diagnosing problems 124
effect of background knowledge
and vocabulary 95, 123
fluency 62, 63–64, 65, 66, 68, 72,
124, 127, 128
goals 125, 130
home reading 4, 61, 73, 128, 130,
151–54
increasing 77–78
for meaning 59–61, 62, 63, 66,
68, 85
mileage 58–59, 125
minimum time to spend
reading 71, 73, 75
pre-teaching 21, 84–85, 89
programme of three kinds of
reading 62–65, 72
receptive knowledge 4, 7, 23, 33,
39, 40, 41, 43, 45, 68
sight vocabulary 23, 32, 39, 117,
147

silent reading 43
speed of reading 63, 64
and spelling 118
teacher vocabulary support 21, 59–61, 84–85, 128
varied receptive meetings with words 44
and vocabulary learning 2, 4, 5, 10–11, 19–21, 22, 23, 24, 27, 28, 36, 39, 70, 73, 75, 123, 124, 125, 131
vocabulary size for 95% and 98% coverage of text 68–70, 74
word families 12, 13
reading aloud 43
to the teacher 128
as vocabulary test 32
Reading Oceans series, Compass Publishing 65–68
recall *see* retrieval
receptive knowledge 18, 23, 33, 39–41, 61, 68, 91
attention 40
elaboration 40, 45
multiple encounters 40, 41, 66–67, 127
noticing 40, 42
retrieval 40, 42, 43, 64, 119, 120
varied meetings and use 40, 44, 45, 64, 94
receptive skills 40
receptive vocabulary size
rate of increase 4, 26–28, 36
testing 29–32, 37
young native speakers of English 25–29, 36, 37
reciprocal reading 63
recycling or re-encountering principle 86, 87, 89, 90, 93, 94, 100, 142
reinforcement 43, 56, 67, 128, 153
repeated reading 64
repetition *see* multiple encounters
re-reading 63, 65, 66, 73, 130, 151
restrictions on the use of words 114–15
retelling 44, 67, 89, 129, 154
retrieval 28, 38, 39–40, 41, 61, 66, 67, 79, 90, 92–93, 94, 100, 118, 119, 142
productive retrieval 40, 42, 43–44, 119, 120
receptive retrieval 40, 42, 43, 64, 119, 120
repeated retrieval 41, 119
rhyming figuratives 108
rich instruction 132
word-focused, using high-frequency vocabulary 139–42
running words 10, 13, 14, 68, 70

scaffolding
discussion 87
intensive reading 128
oral language 48, 49, 71
shared or guided reading 59–61, 128
WordPlosion 133, 135
writing 28
semantic mapping 45–46, 92–94, 95, 138–39
reasons for mapping 157
using pictures 157–58
using words 158
shared or guided reading 39, 59, 62, 72, 75, 127, 130
activity 89–90, 106–07
big book shared reading 61

instructional level 59
  scaffolding for fluency and
    meaning-making 59–61
  vocabulary learning 61–62, 66
sight vocabulary 23, 32, 39, 117, 147
socioeconomic differences, and
    vocabulary size 27–29
speed reading 64
spelling 21, 23, 24, 67, 80, 82, 101
  poor spellers dictionary 101
  rules 115–18, 126
  spelling–sound
    correspondence 116–18, 121–22
spoken language *see* oral language
stems *see* word stems
Storytime Treasure Chest (Radio New
    Zealand) 53, 54
subject-matter teaching and
    learning 21, 24, 28, 77–78, 79,
    85, 89–90
subject-matter vocabulary 15, 24, 85,
    89–90, 126–27
  assessing 35–36
  group brainstorming 137–39
suffixes 8, 12, 18, 21, 22, 80, 102,
    104, 105, 121
  most useful prefixes and
    suffixes 164

teaching vocabulary 5–6, 76, 94–95,
    142
  see also deliberate teaching; rich
    instruction
  analysing deliberate learning
    activities 86–94
  challenges 77–78
  ensuring words are encountered
    many times 79, 83–84
  exercises requiring little or no

attention 81–83
individualisation 77
interference 85–86, 95
intuitions 78
measurement of efficiency 76
positive aspects 78–79
techniques 79–81, 129
test of what every primary teacher
    should know 167–76
topics and activities for an in-
    service course 3
technique feature analysis 46
topic-related vocabulary *see* subject-
    matter vocabulary
transparent compounds 13, 14
true/false tests 31–32

use of words and language 18, 19,
    22–23, 28, 39, 98, 118–19
  see also varied meetings and use of
    words
  activities 106–07, 109
  concepts across cultures 109
  restrictions 114–15
  supported by vocabulary
    knowledge 68–70
  teaching techniques and
    exercises 80–81, 82, 85, 87
  and vocabulary learning 68, 70–72
  word wall 90, 91

varied meetings and use of words 39,
    40, 41, 42, 43, 61–62, 66, 67, 79,
    85, 89, 90, 93, 94, 127, 142
  productive 40, 44–45, 61–62, 64,
    94
  receptive 40, 44, 45, 64, 94
visuals 39, 41–42, 43, 44, 45, 65, 66,
    67, 70, 81, 89–90, 129, 137, 152

Vocabprofiler (VP-Kids) 33–34, 52, 53, 156
vocabulary box or bag 83, 84, 95
vocabulary goals 16–17
vocabulary learning 5, 11, 19–24
   see also contexts of vocabulary knowledge and learning; incidental learning; knowing a word; language-focused learning
   activities and sequences of work 132–42
   applying the conditions 41–46, 72–73, 86–87
   children's books 65–68
   conditions 38–39, 40–41, 46–47, 87, 119–20, 121
   four strands 22, 23, 24, 42, 68, 118
   input supports 70–72
   and language use 68–72, 126–27
   learning goals 29, 77, 78, 84
   learning rate compared to teaching rate 76
   oral language 48–50, 70, 71–72, 73, 78
   reading 61–65, 71, 72, 73, 78
   strategies 21–22, 28
   through movie clips 55–57
vocabulary size 142
   see also Picture Vocabulary Size Test; receptive vocabulary size; Vocabulary Size Test
   closing or narrowing the gap between average and smaller sizes 77, 78
   differences in learners of same age 27–28, 77
   at different age levels 9, 25–28, 49, 124
   estimating 8, 37, 78
   minimum size 29, 78, 147
   needed to get 95% and 98% coverage of text 68–70, 74
   testing 29–36, 37, 124, 131, 149–50
   yes/no test of most frequent 24,000 English words 149–50
vocabulary size, below-average 123–24
   balanced vocabulary development programme 128–30
   diagnosing problems 124, 131
   guidelines for helping learners 124–27
Vocabulary Size Test 9, 33, 36

word card testing 82
word consciousness 4, 5, 21, 23, 94, 96–97, 120, 121, 125–26, 129, 130, 131
   focus activities 97–118, 120–21
   goals 97, 126
   other activities 118–19
word experts 22, 82, 83, 118–19
   steps 165–66
word families 8, 16, 17, 25, 26, 28, 44, 71, 77, 96, 121, 140
   see also Picture Vocabulary Size Test
   activity 102–05
   WordPlosion 133, 134
word family lists 11–14
   examples 12
word frequency *see* frequency
word maps *see* semantic mapping
word parts 18, 19, 20, 21, 23, 24, 39, 46, 70, 82, 85, 92, 96
   see also prefixes; suffixes; word stems
word senses 97–99
word stems 8, 18, 21, 23, 24, 80, 102, 121

activity 105–06
bound stems 102, 105–06
free stems 102
most useful word stems 159–63
word types 16
word wall 83, 90–92
WordPlosion 86, 108, 132–37
writing and written language 5, 8, 18, 19, 20, 23, 27, 28, 33, 39, 40, 67, 127, 128
see also phonics; reading
analysing 33–36
and spelling 118

YouTube 51, 54, 56

Zipf's Law 110, 121

www.ingramcontent.com/pod-product-compliance
Lightning Source LLC
Chambersburg PA
CBHW080806300426
44114CB00020B/2845